D1355841

# GEORDIE MESSIAH

# GEORDIE
# MESSIAH
## The Keegan Years

# ALAN OLIVER

MAINSTREAM
PUBLISHING

EDINBURGH AND LONDON

This book is for my dear mother Betty, my late father Arthur, my wife Judith, son Mark and daughter Suzanne. Their support for my work has helped make writing it possible.

595537

MORAY COUNCIL
Department of Technical
& Leisure Services
796. 334

Copyright © Alan Oliver, 1997
All rights reserved
The moral right of the author has been asserted

First published in Great Britain in 1997 by
MAINSTREAM PUBLISHING COMPANY (EDINBURGH) LTD
7 Albany Street
Edinburgh EH1 3UG

ISBN 1 85158 971 6

No part of this book may be reproduced or transmitted in any form or by any means without written permission from the publisher, except by a reviewer who wishes to quote brief passages in connection with a review written for insertion in a magazine, newspaper or broadcast

A catalogue record for this book is available from the British Library

Typeset in Plantin
Printed and bound in Great Britain by Butler and Tanner Ltd, Frome

# CONTENTS

# ACKNOWLEDGEMENTS

Ian Murtagh, *The Journal*
Mark Oliver, Mirror Group Newspapers
Alison Hastings, Editor, *Evening Chronicle*
Paul New, Sports Editor, *Evening Chronicle*, and his staff
John Stokoe, *United Magazine*, and his staff
Paul Joannou and Steve Corke, Newcastle United Statisticians

# 1

## KEEGAN QUITS

WHEN THE NEWS broke it wasn't unexpected. But that still did not lessen the shock. Within the hour the tears were flooding into the River Tyne. Fans besieged the *Evening Chronicle* offices in the heart of the City. 'Tell us it isn't true,' they wailed. But it was. The newspaper billboards for once told the whole story: Keegan quits.

Tyneside came to a standstill. It was the only topic of conversation in the offices and shops and in the giant MetroCentre built by Keegan's own Chairman, Sir John Hall. Some members of the Toon Army wore black armbands. One fan had a black tombstone tattooed on his right arm with the message 'R.I.P. Kevin Keegan 92–97 N.U.F.C.'.

Others headed to St James's Park as though it was their Mecca. They thought by going there they could make their hero change his mind. But it was too late. Keegan had already been at St James's Park 24 hours earlier and, like so many United managers before him, wistfully and reluctantly cleared his desk.

The mood on Tyneside was sombre. It was as if everyone had suffered a family bereavement. The personalities queued up to pay their tributes. First Labour leader Tony Blair. Then Prime Minister and Chelsea supporter John Major. The word reverberated around the world. It was the big news in every country where football is played and even in countries where it is not. Yet for those who worked with Kevin Keegan it was no surprise that the King had abdicated. The signs had been there for so long.

Every Newcastle United supporter had felt the pain as the Geordies allowed Manchester United to gnaw away at that 12-point lead the season before, when Alex Ferguson's side finally took the Premiership title. But the pain was a lot worse for Keegan. He was the focal point of the whole club. He carried the can, especially when things went wrong. His outburst against Alex Ferguson after the game at Leeds, three games off the end of the season, was beamed out live by Sky Television and played back countless times to demonstrate the pressure and stress Keegan was under.

Newcastle's last game of the 1995–96 season was against Spurs at St James's Park on Sunday, 5 May. It was still possible for Keegan to win the Premiership title for United, his adoring supporters and Sir John Hall and his board. Yet the night before Keegan had talked about resigning with the club's directors. It was all denied the day after, before the Spurs match. But all this came to light when the United directors accepted his resignation eight months later.

Newcastle could only draw with Spurs, but it didn't matter whether they won or not, for down the coast on Teesside Manchester United beat Middlesbrough to claim the Premiership title. Yet back at St James's Park you would have thought Newcastle had won the championship, judging from the reception Keegan and his players received from the United supporters. There was one heck of a party in Newcastle's Bigg Market that night and the feeling was that if this is what it's like when Newcastle finish runners-up, what is it going to be like when they win the championship?

Significantly, Keegan did not attend the post-match press conference after the Spurs game, although the Premiership hierarchy frown on this, and in the close season, Keegan decided that he would no longer see the media on a daily basis as he had from the moment he returned in February 1992. Instead, Keegan decreed that he would only see the media immediately before and after the game. But it was when he refused to face the press after the humiliating defeat at Coventry on 17 December that things started to get really bad.

I was talking to Coventry's Geordie-born midfielder Kevin Richardson in the corridors beside the dressing-rooms when Keegan walked past. He didn't look particularly angry. Certainly, I have seen him look a lot angrier. But instead of turning right and up the stairs into the press room, he turned left and out on to the team bus. I knew then that the Midland press would have a field day at the expense of the Newcastle manager.

It had been a particularly bad night for Keegan and Newcastle. Coventry were bottom of the league, yet they won 2–1. Darren Huckerby, whom Keegan had sold to Coventry only a month earlier, scored the first goal early on and made the second for Gary McAllister after half an hour. Keegan knew that he would have to fend off questions about Huckerby. He could have done it. I've seen him do this on countless occasions. There were so many times in his time as manager of Newcastle United that he faced a hostile press away from St James's Park and charmed them out of the trees. But at Highfield Road that freezing December night, he decided in his wisdom not to face the press. He must have known what the consequences were. 'Keegan storms out' made better headlines than the actual match. Morose. Stony-faced. These were some of the descriptions of Keegan the next day.

To make matters worse, United's plans to get away from their Highfield Road torture chamber were thwarted. The United team bus was blocked in for 20 minutes and they had to sit there fuming until the offending car owner was found and they could head back up the motorway.

After Coventry, United entertained Liverpool six days later and just two days before Christmas. It was a splendid match between two excellent teams and ended 1–1. After the game the general feeling was that Keegan had been no way like his normal self. In the press conference, media men who had worked with him felt that he had only gone through the motions. He was subdued. Almost depressed.

But if any one match swayed Keegan to the decision that he no longer wanted to be manager of Newcastle United, then that match was undoubtedly the Boxing Day defeat by Blackburn Rovers at Ewood Park. In a subdued United dressing-room after the game Keegan really let rip into his players as he had never done before.

It was another bad night all round for United. Keegan had made Alan Shearer captain for his return to Blackburn. Shearer was jeered by the fans who had once worshipped him and he was booked. Then late in the game Kevin Gallacher got the goal which gave Blackburn a 1–0 win. On the whistle all the pressmen headed in my direction. 'Will your man come in?' they taunted me. Well, they soon got their answer. Like a lot of clubs, Blackburn have an auditorium-type room next to the press room and Keegan was in there before most of the press had finished their match reports. Consequently there were only a handful of press present when Keegan eased himself into his seat, and the press conference was laboured to say the least. There were embarrassing long silences from both parties. Keegan gave one-word answers to some questions. After one long pause Keegan chided the press. He told them he got into trouble for not attending press conferences, yet here he was and there was hardly a question put before him.

I have never asked questions in the main press conference because they are all out of evening newspaper time, and it was no good to me if the answers were in the morning papers. Before the 1996–97 season Keegan usually gave the evening paper men a couple of minutes on their own. But under the new press regulations, written in stone by Keegan, this was no longer done. However, I felt I had to have a go on this occasion, and as he left the auditorium I asked if he would give me a couple of minutes outside. He indicated he would. But when I got outside I found that Keegan was walking towards the lift. I chased after him and asked if David Ginola would be fit for the game with Spurs on the Saturday. His response was, 'I haven't a clue, Alan, I haven't a clue.' As he got into the lift he answered my query as to why Warren Barton was not at the ground, informing me that the full-back had been so ill he had been left at the team's hotel.

After that he was gone. I never spoke to Kevin Keegan again, even though he was to be manager of Newcastle United for another 13 days. I have known Keegan a long time as a player and a manager but I have never seen him as low as he was that Boxing Day night at Ewood Park. There was a report the next day that there had been a couple of shouts from the Newcastle fans of 'Keegan out', but I never heard them. However, I felt there and then that it was not beyond the realms of possibility that Keegan would walk away from it all.

I bumped into Vice-Chairman Freddie Shepherd and Director Douglas Hall after the Blackburn game as they left Ewood Park. They were usually full of it – usually a joke at my expense. However, on this occasion they were both tight-lipped as they got into their car to drive home. I felt uneasy the next day and I had every right to be. I tried ringing club officials, but none was available. And it became clear why later on. For on the Friday after the Boxing Day defeat Keegan summoned the Newcastle top brass to his Wynyard home and told them he wanted to quit. Once again the directors talked him out of it.

The following day, Newcastle met Spurs at St James's Park. United had failed to win any of their previous seven Premiership games but while there had been odd letters in the local sports pages which were beginning to criticise Keegan, the fans were still wholeheartedly behind their charismatic manager. Spurs were ideal opposition that day. They are notoriously bad travellers and they were without several key men because of injuries. My colleagues in the press room laughed at me when I slipped a couple of quid on United to win 4–0. They laughed even louder when Philippe Albert made it 5–0, as Newcastle went on to a resounding 7–1 win.

This was the perfect opportunity for Keegan to face the press, but once again there was no sign of him. Instead his right-hand man Terry McDermott appeared to say that Keegan had rushed home because his wife Jean was ill. Not surprisingly there were some press men who were cynical about this excuse.

The fans were also beginning to sense something was wrong. Although the BBC did not highlight it when Robert Lee scored United's fourth goal against Spurs, there was no reaction from Keegan. This was not the Kevin Keegan the supporters knew and loved. John Regan of the Independent Newcastle Supporters Association contacted me to say the fans were appalled at some of the letters which were beginning to appear criticising Keegan.

The arrival of another New Year saw Leeds United at St James's Park. George Graham's side were dispatched 3–0. I had become friendly with Graham because of Keegan. In my Pink column a couple of years earlier I had written that 'dour Scots'

Alex Ferguson and Graham could take a leaf out of Keegan's book in his open dealings with the press. Graham, who was the overlord at Arsenal, stopped a press conference at Highbury to chastise me. But when he was out of the game and doing some press work we became friends. That's probably why Graham pulled me up at St James's Park after the Leeds game and asked just what was going on with the criticism of Keegan. He told me Alex Ferguson must have been laughing all the way to the Old Trafford trophy room. I could not have agreed more.

But it was a big friend of Keegan's, our press room tea lady, who really opened my eyes on New Year's Day. Kath Cassidy loves Kevin Keegan, just like she loved Newcastle United's other legend, Jackie Milburn. In the few minutes she saw him after every home game, Kath could see how distressed Keegan had become. Before every game Kath takes out her framed photograph of the late and great Wor Jackie and places it on the press room wall. It was when she was taking Jackie's picture down that Kath said to me, 'Alan, what can we do about our manager, he's so unhappy?' Keegan's parting shot to Kath that New Year's Day had been, 'I love coming in here to see you. I don't like coming in to see this other lot.'

Normally this would have brought the house down, and been greeted with laughter by the press boys who loved Keegan's quips and one-liners. But there was no laughter on this occasion. The press felt that Keegan really meant it. By now there was a lot of talk that Keegan had offered to quit and had been persuaded to stay by the United directors. Only Brian McNally in the *Sunday Mirror* felt confident that he had enough information – and the courage – to write it.

So, on Sunday, 5 January, the *Sunday Mirror* ran a 'Keegan quits' story. Newcastle were in a freezing South London that day for a televised FA Cup third-round tie with Charlton Athletic at The Valley. Not surprisingly Sky brought up the 'Keegan quits' story. But there was no comment from Newcastle for the television cameras, either before or after the game. At the end of the match, again the talk was whether Keegan would come into the press conference, especially as news filtered through that he had refused to go on Sky Television. Suddenly the word spread like wildfire that Keegan was on his way.

Now Charlton's press room is not up to Premiership standards. It's a little portakabin in the The Valley car park. Keegan, as barrel-chested as ever, strode towards it with his press officer Graham Courtney. Deep down Keegan must have known he would be asked about the *Sunday Mirror* story. I don't know if that is why he did not enter the portakabin but stood at the doorway as if to make a quick getaway. Keegan was more like his old self as he talked about the match. He seemed relaxed and had the South London press boys laughing at some of his renowned one-liners. But I knew this was just the calm before the storm. You could have cut the tension in the air with a knife.

It's an old press trick to ask the most damaging question last of all, and with the other guys stalling a bit it was left to the Press Association's Martin Lipton to ask the big one. Lipton tried to ease into it, suggesting to Keegan that he had woken up to headlines proclaiming that he was thinking of quitting. Keegan tried to brush it aside, saying that he thought he had come to the press conference to talk about the match. But as he turned on his heels he fumed, 'You know the guy who wrote it. End of story.' I don't know whether Keegan heard it but he was cat-called and jeered as he stormed away. I must say that this hurt me, for I knew more than anyone just how magnificent Keegan had been with the press.

But I also knew the guy who wrote the story. Brian McNally has won more awards than any other journalist around these days. In fact, McNally probably has more journalistic awards than Keegan has managerial honours. I knew that he must have been pretty sure of himself to have written his story as strongly as he did. Newcastle had Graham Courtney, Vice-Chairman Freddie Shepherd, Chief Executive Freddie Fletcher and General Manager Russell Cushing with them at The Valley, but there was no official comment from any of them. Or perhaps, more significantly, no official denial.

The following day I ran a comment piece saying that if a Newcastle manager had offered to quit no matter who he was it was big news, and that the supporters were entitled to know. But there was still no comment, official or otherwise, from United. And the next day, Tuesday, 7 January, I did a sports page lead backed up with revealing statistics to point out that on results

Kevin Keegan was the most successful manager in the history of Newcastle United, even though he had not won any silverware. It was a fair point, but Keegan had already made up his mind. There was no going back.

At 11.30 that night I took a call informing me that Keegan had actually quit. I had a sleepless night worrying whether the story had already been broken in the morning papers. It hadn't. Surprisingly there was hardly a word about the Keegan managerial situation in the morning papers of Wednesday, 8 January. I was at my desk at 6.30 a.m. I immediately typed one sentence into my computer – 'Kevin Keegan sensationally resigned today as manager of Newcastle United.' But because of the silence from the club I did not type another word for three hours.

Alison Hastings, the Editor of the *Evening Chronicle*, and Sports Editor Paul New were soon put in the picture. They informed their staff, and the whole of the *Evening Chronicle* was ready for action. If it was right, it would probably be the biggest story the *Evening Chronicle* would ever get. But it wasn't easy to crack. Even before 8 a.m., my old pal Vic Wakeling, who is the head of Sky Sports, and whom I know as we both lived in Consett, was on the phone. He had tried to speak to both United Vice-Chairman Freddie Shepherd and Chief Executive Freddie Fletcher. But he could not get through to either. Considering the amount of money Sky Television has put into football, Vic Wakeling has a lot of influence. He was concerned that he had been unable to contact Messrs Shepherd or Fletcher. He asked me what was going on. He knew that if it was the big one he had to get his cameras up to Newcastle, and mighty quickly at that. But the silence coming out of St James's Park was almost deafening.

However, bits and pieces started to come together. I had a man at United's training ground at Durham. He told me that when the United players arrived for training, Terry McDermott pulled them to one side. I knew then that something big had happened for Terry Mac to do this. It could only be that Keegan had resigned. At this point we decided to go with it. The *Evening Chronicle* was galvanised into action. Almost to a man – and woman – they are Newcastle United fans. And Keegan fans. Like everyone else they were stunned and shocked, but they all did a superb professional job, a fact later acknowledged by Alison Hastings and Executive Editor Neil Benson. As I was tapping in the story, the official confirmaton finally came from Graham Courtney. The *Evening Chronicle* had held back its first edition, but we were soon on the streets. Soon the telephone calls came in from all over the world.

The atmosphere in Newcastle was sombre. It was unreal. Fans said they felt as though there had been a death in the family. It wasn't until later that I realised the personal side of it all. Kevin Keegan had quit Newcastle United on 8 January – the same day as my own father had died in 1980. It was also two years to the day since he had sold Andy Cole to Manchester United.

The tributes flowed in as soon as the news broke that Keegan had resigned, especially from the heartbroken fans. Every one was genuine. Some were sad. Some were even funny. The wittiest undoubtedly came from the supporter who said, 'To see someone else in charge of Newcastle United will be like watching wor lass (*my wife*) in bed with another bloke.'

After the resignation there were only two questions. Why did he quit? And who was going to take over? Now everyone on Tyneside has an opinion on football. I remember Jim Smith saying to me when he was the manager of Newcastle, 'What chance have I here when there are 20,000 internationals sitting in the stands?' So, not surprisingly, everyone had an opinion on just why Keegan had walked out on the job and club he loved.

Fans. Stress experts. Psychiatrists. Former players. Fellow managers. The media. Uncle Tom Cobbleigh and all. They all had their say. But Keegan and Newcastle United stayed silent, apart from one initial and curt statement. The physical signs had been there for some time. When he arrived back at Newcastle the hair was jet black. Yet in every one of his five seasons his hair became greyer and greyer. It seemed to make him feel better that my hair had become whiter and whiter. And he loved telling me so. Keegan's handsome features gave way to wrinkles, and heavy bags developed under his eyes. But all the experts agreed on one thing – it was the mental pressure which caused Keegan to quit.

I've lost count of the number of people who have come up to me and asked me the real or hidden reasons why Keegan had walked away from the job he had all but finished. My answer is that there is no hidden reason as far as I know. What I do know is that Keegan desperately wanted to win something for the Geordie fans. It was almost an obsession. There is no doubt that Keegan was and still is a perfectionist. His own standards as a man, husband, father, footballer and manager were so high that it was always going to be nearly impossible for 11 individuals to match them on a Saturday afternoon.

He wasn't just happy with winning. He wanted to win with style. When United did not do this, the pressure gradually built up inside of him. But it was pressure that he created himself. There was absolutely no pressure from the Newcastle United board. They remembered only too well the mess the club was in when he arrived, and United's long-suffering supporters had even more vivid memories of the bad old days. Just before Keegan arrived, Newcastle United were humiliated by Southend. With respect, they should not have been on the same field as Newcastle United. Yet just before Keegan left, Newcastle United handed out a 5–0 drubbing to Manchester United. I don't go along with any theories that the money men, with the club's flotation imminent, had anything to do with Keegan's decision.

Kevin Keegan could have stayed as manager of Newcastle United. The decision to go was his and his alone. He said his decision was in the best interests of Newcastle United Football Club, and when Kegan said something, people did not usually argue. However, the arguments as to why Keegan did resign will go on for a long time yet. Only one man knows the real reasons: Kevin Keegan.

When Keegan did speak it was in his column in *The Sun* on 7 February – two days after he should have been celebrating five years as manager of Newcastle United, and nearly a month after he resigned. But it was all very much an anti-climax. In fact, it was all pretty tame stuff. Keegan pinpointed the look on the face of Spurs manager Gerry Francis as United walloped his side 7–1 at St James's Park just after Christmas as one of the reasons why he left.

Keegan said that the elation of winning suddenly meant nothing to him. The reaction from the Newcastle fans to

Keegan's revelations was in the main disappointment. Steve Wraith, Editor of the fast-rising *No. 9* fanzine, claimed that it still wasn't any clearer why Keegan had gone and said that he had seemed to have sidetracked from what the true story was. Wraith called for Keegan to give a fuller explanation to the United supporters on just why he had quit. But in general there were few complaints from the fans.

They knew that no matter what he said, he wasn't coming back.

# 2

## KEEGAN THE PLAYER

NEWCASTLE UNITED got something from Kevin Keegan that nobody else got. A double dose: Keegan the player and Keegan the manager. It made life doubly exciting for both the fans and the media.

When Keegan the player arrived at St James's Park things weren't quite as bad as when he answered that SOS to take over as manager. But life was still pretty dull for everyone concerned with the club before Kevin joined United from Southampton in the summer of 1982.

Certainly, speaking from the press point of view, Keegan transformed our professional lives – twice. The *Evening Chronicle* decided I was the man for them in 1980 because I was one of the few people who could hit it off with the then manager Bill McGarry. But I only worked with McGarry for three weeks before he was sacked – and the start of 1996–97 marked my 17th season covering the fortunes of Newcastle for the *Chronicle*.

McGarry was replaced by Arthur Cox, someone I've enjoyed a love-hate relationship with over the years. Cox was to become one of the game's leading figures but in those days his appointment hardly pulled up many trees. The Chesterfield manager resigned to take over at the club which had finished halfway in the old Second Division – big deal. Of course, if it moved at Newcastle, the *Evening Chronicle* covered it and, despite the fact crowds regularly dipped below 18,000, we would treat any signing as world-shattering news. It was what our readers had come to expect. So when the likes of Peter Johnson, Imre Varadi or Mick Hartford joined United, the sports desk went to town with interviews, career details and comment.

Johnson was Cox's first signing. He spent £60,000 on the Boro left-back – quite a fee for a club pleading poverty. As if to emphasise the transformation in Newcastle's fortunes, when Keegan took his squad out to the Far East in July 1996, £60,000 was the cost of United's laundry bill for the tour. In 1981, however, you'd need a magnifying glass to find news of any moves to St James's Park in the nationals. Quite simply, for all their proud tradition, Newcastle United didn't matter as far as the London boys who decided what went in the newspapers were concerned. That all changed in August 1982. Thanks to Kevin Keegan, my job suddenly became one of the most high profile in sports journalism.

I've got a confession to make. Back then, I'd become conditioned into believing Newcastle were incapable of competing for the biggest names in football. There'd been some decent stories over the years – the emergence of Chris Waddle, a former sausage factory worker who'd played for Tow Law in the Northern League, John Trewick's record-breaking transfer – a whopping £250,000 (which wasn't to be broken for seven years), Alan Brown's on-off move from Sunderland and Varadi's goal-scoring exploits. But United had that nasty habit of kicking you in the teeth just when they looked as if they might do something. The 1980–81 season provided the classic example. Quite frankly, that was a desperate campaign, perfectly illustrated by the fact that Bobby Shinton ended up the club's top scorer with a grand total of seven goals. But with Waddle in inspirational form, Newcastle had overcome Sheffield Wednesday and Luton in the FA Cup and now had another home draw against unfashionable Exeter City. All of a sudden, a quarter-final place was on the horizon for the first time since 1976.

What happened? Newcastle were held to a 1–1 draw at Gallowgate and in the replay at the other St James's Park, the Devon side thrashed a woeful United 4–0. It was probably the low point of my time on the black and white beat.

So when, 18 months later, I spotted a story written by Vince Wilson in the *Sunday Mirror*, I didn't take too much notice. Rumours had been rife that Keegan wanted to quit Southampton despite his goal-scoring exploits at The Dell the previous year. But Newcastle United? I couldn't understand why Wilson had dropped in that name. After all, Manchester United were in the race to sign the England captain. He wouldn't turn down the Old Trafford giants for Newcastle, would he?

Keegan was Britain's most famous footballer since Manchester United's George Best, but his career had humble beginnings. The Doncaster-born forward had started out with Fourth Division Scunthorpe before joining Liverpool on the eve of the 1971 FA Cup final. Arsenal won that match 2–1 in extra time to clinch the 'double' and deny the Anfield side their first Wembley victory since 1965.

When Liverpool did win the Cup, it was against Newcastle United and KK was their chief executioner, scoring two second-half goals in a game which was to be the legendary Bill Shankly's last in charge. United were an embarrassment that day, losing 3–0. If the 1974 showpiece went down in the history books as one of the most one-sided in the history of the competition, Keegan's career was about to take off. His partnership with John Toshack proved one of the most potent ever seen at Liverpool, with both players' goal tallies reaching double figures four seasons in a row.

But by 1977, football's first millionaire was seeking pastures new and with Liverpool chasing honours on three fronts, he announced he'd be moving abroad in the summer. Fittingly, Keegan inspired a side, now managed by Bob Paisley, to Championship glory and they were overwhelming favourites to win the FA Cup too, only for arch-rivals Manchester United to beat them 2–1 in the final.

A few days later Liverpool flew out to Rome to meet Borussia Monchengladbach in the European Cup final. Despite their domestic success and a UEFA Cup triumph in 1973, Europe's most glittering prize had eluded Liverpool during Shankly's reign but on a glorious night Keegan turned in one of his best-ever performances in a red shirt. It was team-mate Terry McDermott, later to become one of his closest confidants, who opened the scoring and after the Germans had levelled, veteran Tommy Smith scored one of his rare goals, a bullet header which restored Liverpool's advantage. Then came Keegan's *pièce de résistance*. Twisting and turning in a mesmerising run into the opposition penalty area, he tormented Berti Vogts to such an extent that one of Europe's finest man-markers was forced to concede a penalty. Up stepped Phil Neal to make it 3–1 and the Cup was Liverpool's. Keegan's last match for his beloved Reds had provided the appropriate swansong. So it was on to Germany and Gunter Netzer's Hamburg, a team struggling to break the Borussia/Bayern Munich duopoly.

By this time, Keegan was sporting a new-look perm. A role model for thousands, this distinctly '70s-style hairstyle was to set a trend for years to come. A pop record, 'Head Over Heels', earned him an appearance on *Top of the Pops*. On or off the pitch, it seemed, everything he touched turned to gold.

But Keegan's early months in northern Germany were not easy. There was talk of jealousy among his team-mates, his young daughter Laura was ill and on the pitch results were mediocre. But such was the innate determination of the man, his time abroad catapulted him towards the pinnacle of his profession. He mastered the language, won over the doubters and helped Hamburg to the title. Nicknamed Mickey Mouse by his adoring disciples, Keegan was now recognised as the Continent's most outstanding footballer. It was during his spell abroad that England boss Ron Greenwood appointed him captain and he won the European Footballer of the Year award in successive years.

The one disappointment during his time at Hamburg was that he failed to become one of the few players to win the European Cup with two clubs. Ironically, it was English outfit Nottingham Forest who denied him such an honour with John Robertson scoring the only goal of the 1979 final as Brian Clough's side retained the trophy.

Keegan's next move was a surprise. He could have had his pick of any club but chose unfashionable Southampton, largely due to the influence of his friend Lawrie McMenemy, the Saints' big Geordie boss. KK didn't win any honours during his time on the south coast but, if anything, he was at the height of his powers.

Though a regular goal-scorer for many years, he could never had been described as prolific. But in 1981–82, Keegan proved himself a sharpshooter to match the best, scoring 26 goals in 41 league outings as Southampton finished runners-up in the First Division. With an idyllic lifestyle in Hampshire, Keegan could have spent the rest of his career at The Dell but at 30 he wanted a new challenge and they didn't come much bigger than Newcastle United.

The summer of 1982 hadn't been the best of times for Keegan. Denied appearances in the World Cup finals of 1974 and 1978 due to England's failure to qualify, he had done more than anyone to ensure Greenwood's team would be figuring in the tournament in Spain. But a persistent back injury meant he was unavailable for England's three group matches and despite a rigorous fitness programme, he also sat out the match against Germany in the second stage. By the time England faced Spain, they knew only a win would secure progress into the semi-finals. Keegan and Trevor Brooking were on the bench that day and that's probably where they would have stayed had their team-mates been able to transfer their superiority into goals. But with time running out, the situation was becoming desperate and so Keegan and Brooking were thrown into the fray. There was to be no fairy tale though. Keegan, normally so clinical with his head despite a lack of inches, wasted a glorious chance late on to snatch a dramatic winner. For the first time in his footballing life, KK was the villain of the hour.

Within weeks, however, Keegan was in more familiar territory, being hero-worshipped by thousands of new-found fans on Tyneside. Talks between the two parties had been more straightforward than the club hierarchy had anticipated. 'The moment I met Newcastle's officials and shook hands, I knew that was it. I only talked to Manchester United and Newcastle. I knew Newcastle wanted me and I had not felt so excited in a long time, since I first met Bill Shankly in fact.'

Keegan's love affair with United began on 19 August 1982: 'We're in heaven, we've got Kevin,' announced Newcastle United secretary Russell Cushing at the press conference to welcome his arrival. Indeed they were but success wouldn't be immediate for new-look United.

Nothing quite captures Keegan's aura more than his pulling power. Just four months before his Magpies debut against Queen's Park Rangers at St James's Park, United had attracted a woeful crowd of 10,670 against the same opposition – and lost 4–0. There was little chance of history repeating itself nor of the crowd being so small. Season ticket sales had increased almost ten-fold in the wake of the sensational announcement and on the big day itself, fans started queuing at 6 a.m., including a teenage Alan Shearer. It wasn't just the 36,000 inside the ground and the thousands locked out who had been attracted back to Tyneside's citadel, Fleet Street hacks who hadn't travelled this far north in a decade converged on St James's.

Rangers were a good team – destined for promotion that year – but the script demanded they were merely bit-part players on this occasion. Keegan had emerged from the tunnel to deafening cheers clad in a white sweat-shirt and the decibel count soared as he stripped off his top to reveal the famous black and white shirt. At last, those fans, brought up on a diet of false promises and broken dreams, could witness glorious reality. The match was no classic but Keegan inevitably ensured it would be a memorable one. In the second half, latching on to a flick-on from Imre Varadi, he surged through the inside-right channel before driving a low shot past the diving Peter Hucker. The love affair was then consummated as United's new skipper kept on running towards the dancing Gallowgate hordes. It was fully two minutes before the visitors could restart the game but they were powerless to prevent Newcastle securing a 1–0 win. When Keegan scored again in a 2–1 victory over Blackburn at Ewood Park four days later – the travelling fans swelling Rovers' gate to 14,421 – it seemed the United bandwagon may prove unstoppable.

But Newcastle were not equipped to challenge for promotion that season and a 3–1 defeat at Bolton emphasised the fact that surgery was still required if the club were going to exploit the Keegan phenomenon. And so the likes of Steve Hardwick, Peter Cartwright, Peter Haddock and John Craggs, who lost his place to John Anderson despite only joining United that summer, soon found themselves out in the cold. Keegan was followed into St James's by his former Liverpool team-mate Terry McDermott who had quit United for his boyhood favourites eight years earlier. When the pair combined brilliantly to set up a stunning 5–1 win at Rotherham on 2 October, it seemed as if Cox had discovered the missing combination. Once again, that result proved a false dawn, ruthlessly emphasised by Malcolm Macdonald's Fulham who performed brilliantly a week later to win 4–1 at his former stamping ground in front of the *Match of the Day* cameras.

After so many years reporting a team going nowhere, the 1982–83 campaign was a breath of fresh air for the press, even if Newcastle were struggling for consistency on the pitch. There were some wonderful stories to write, like the time Terry Mac dressed up as an Arab sheikh and approached Cox informing him that Keegan was wanted by one of the richest clubs in the Middle East who were prepared to pay a king's ransom for his signature. Guess who'd been behind that practical joke? Then there was the occasion when the dynamic duo decided to take their revenge on Cox, who had developed a reputation as one of the toughest taskmasters around when it came to training. One Tuesday at a training session at Newcastle's former Benwell site, Keegan and McDermott were nowhere to be seen. Cox was becoming worried for it wasn't like those two ultra-professionals to go missing. Suddenly, in the distance, the manager spotted two figures charging towards him dressed from head to toe in army gear. The pair had decided to dress up as SAS commandos. It was their way of telling Cox his sergeant-major image was going a bit too far!

Paul Gascoigne never played in the same team as Keegan. His debut arrived ten months after Kevin had quit football, but that didn't stop the precocious youngster leaving a lasting impression on the Newcastle skipper. As an apprentice, Gascoigne was assigned the task of cleaning Keegan's boots. Now Gazza being Gazza couldn't resist telling his mates in Dunston that he had been chosen out of all the kids at Newcastle to perform such a key task for the great man. Unfortunately, they didn't believe him, so one day Gascoigne decided to take a pair home to provide concrete proof – and promptly lost the boots by leaving them on the bus. The 16-year-old was petrified of the consequences when Keegan found out so he broached the subject rather tentatively. He needn't have worried. Keegan, arms round the lovable Geordie, took him to the St James's Park boot-room and showed him more than a dozen identical pairs all belonging to him. One lost pair wasn't going to upset a player the sponsors were falling over themselves to endorse.

Keegan's presence was ensuring Newcastle would never be out of the limelight. His close friend Mick Channon joined the club's ever-increasing galaxy of stars, though his stay was to be cut short. Then David McCreery, a tough-tackling midfielder, who was to become a huge favourite with the Toon Army, was recruited.

The autumn, however, was not a happy time for Keegan. New England boss Bobby Robson, a self-confessed Newcastle fan, had watched his skipper score on his United debut. In international terms, it looked a marriage made in heaven. But Robson controversially axed England's most famous player from his first squad, abruptly ending his distinguished career at this level without warning Keegan beforehand. The deposed captain felt betrayed, hurt and humiliated and didn't mind who knew it. Robson, sadly, became a figure of hate among United fans, and on subsequent visits to the region, his presence was greeted by concerted booing. I couldn't help recalling that unsavoury episode in the days following Keegan's resignation. It would be fair to say that the rift, though never properly healed, was never really an issue once KK hung up his boots. When it became obvious that Barcelona boss Robson was Chairman Sir John Hall's choice to replace Keegan, I knew of several fans who disapproved because of his snub almost a decade earlier.

Keegan's second setback was more damaging to Newcastle United. Playing in a testimonial game for Middlesbrough's Darren Wood at Ayresome Park, he sustained a freak eye injury. It kept him sidelined for five games. Not surprisingly, the team won just one of those fixtures. Even on his reappearance, Newcastle remained on the periphery of the promotion race, drawing three successive games 2–2 over the festive period when Liverpool's Howard Gayle spent a brief spell on loan.

If Newcastle weren't quite good enough for the First Division, they looked a good bet for a decent run in the FA Cup. Even Bob Wilson of the BBC's *Football Focus* tipped them as potential winners. The Cup, however, was to provide Keegan with some of his most frustrating nights in a black and white shirt. A 1–1 draw against Brighton at the Goldstone Ground was a good start – with the replay expected to be a formality for United. But it didn't quite work out that way – largely due to a referee from Barnsley called Trelford Mills whose name will forever be linked with United's Cup exit in 1983. The Seagulls had taken a shock lead but with Newcastle bombarding the visitors' goal, it seemed only a matter of time before their superiority eventually paid off. But Mills controversially ruled out two goals – by Steve Carney and Imre Varadi – decisions which not only stunned the home fans but led to furious protests from the Newcastle players led by their skipper. Keegan had a fine disciplinary record during his career but that night, in my opinion, he came perilously close to being sent off, such was his reaction to Mills' handling of the Cup-tie.

In the league, Newcastle scored in every game between 4 December and 30 April but their best came too late. With Chris Waddle suddenly finding his form after being initially overawed following Keegan's arrival, and both Keegan and Varadi scoring regularly, Newcastle became a force on home soil. They beat Shrewsbury, Grimsby and Rotherham 4–0 and also picked up maximum points against Oldham, Leeds, Blackburn and Charlton. Going into the closing stages, four successive wins made them promotion dark horses until a 1–0 defeat at Cambridge, of all places, effectively aborted their challenge.

But there was to be a dramatic finale to the campaign. A 5–0 rout of Barnsley at Oakwell, with Keegan, Varadi (two) and Neil McDonald (two) scoring the goals, meant that if Newcastle could win their last two games and Leicester City or Wolves slipped up, they could yet squeeze into the top three. At St James's Park on 7 May rumours swept across the ground that results elsewhere were in Newcastle's favour and with the hosts leading Sheffield Wednesday 2–1, all of a sudden the impossible seemed possible. It was not to be, however, as it became obvious the crowd had been misinformed. United were destined to spend another 12 months outside the top flight – not that it prevented the fans from celebrating a memorable season on the final whistle. Newcastle may have failed in their prime objective but those scenes were a welcome change from the apathy which had greeted the curtain coming down on previous campaigns.

If supporters delivered a positive verdict on proceedings, though, this was not reciprocated by Keegan. Though he was clearly relishing life at United, from a personal point of view, the move to the North-East did present difficulties. Indeed wife Jean and his two young daughters were still based at their Hampshire home with the breadwinner splitting his life between the Gosforth Park Hotel on the outskirts of Newcastle and home. In truth, however, this was never going to be a major problem for the Keegans. It was a football-related matter which cast a shadow over his immediate future at St James's Park. Newcastle United was to be his last club and he didn't want to be associated with failure at this stage in his career. And so, before he put pen to paper on a new one-year contract, Keegan sought reassurances from Chairman Stan Seymour and Cox. Clearly, Newcastle United had not been good enough to achieve a top three slot in the Second Division and Keegan felt that for them to progress in the months ahead he needed to be surrounded by better players. 'I'm not holding a gun to their head but I want to see some movement from the club,' he said. The message was clear. Only promotion would satisfy Keegan in 1983–84 and his new contract reflected that with a series of escape clauses inserted in the event of the campaign petering out.

Fifteen years earlier, another cult hero, Pop Robson, had slammed the United hierarchy, labelling them 'unprofessional', and his departure to West Ham left a sour taste in the mouth. But Keegan was different. Not only was he articulating the feeling among fans, but when he talked the directors listened. Keegan was probably the only player in my experience who could have got away with what he said. Cox and his skipper were on the same wavelength but it required a constructive outburst from Keegan rather than the manager to ensure United did build on the previous term's platform.

And so the squad was duly strengthened. Keeper Martin Thomas, who had been on loan, signed on a permanent basis, while full-backs Malcolm Brown and John Ryan were signed from Huddersfield and Oldham respectively. The pair were rated among the best attack-minded defenders outside the top flight, with many experts predicting an international future ahead for

Ryan. As it turned out, neither was to make much of an impact at Newcastle. The hapless Brown, who had hardly missed a game for Huddersfield, suffered a freak pre-season injury and didn't play at all that season while Ryan struggled to come to terms with life at a high-profile club at Newcastle and was eventually axed in favour of the loyal Kenny Wharton. Nevertheless, the message was clear. Newcastle were prepared to spend in a bid to win promotion. The fans were excited – and Keegan was satisfied.

That grassroots optimism was shattered a few days before the big kick-off. Varadi had been a huge favourite among the masses, his goals, particularly in the year before Keegan's arrival, bringing some much-needed excitement to Gallowgate. Admittedly, his touch wasn't the best but Varadi's blistering pace and ability to score spectacular goals brought back memories of Malcolm Macdonald. Keegan, however, didn't relish the prospect of another campaign alongside a player whose lack of technique often led to moves breaking down. Brought up at the Anfield passing school, KK liked the ball played to his feet and was at his best alongside strikers who could control a ball and lay it off with the minimum of fuss. Varadi was a 100-miles-per-hour forward who loved nothing better than chasing a long punt over the top. As far as Keegan was concerned, despite his team-mate's goals' return, the partnership didn't have a future.

Supporters were aghast when Varadi was packed off to Sheffield Wednesday, even more so when it became clear he wanted to stay. And though Newcastle kicked off the campaign with an impressive victory against Leeds at Elland Road – when the unsung John Anderson bagged the winner and Waddle finished the game in goal – their frustration spilled over two days later when United inexplicably lost at home to Shrewsbury. Poor David Mills was the fans' scapegoat that Bank Holiday afternoon as he was perceived to be the man who would replace Varadi.

But the wily Cox had yet to show his winning hand. Keegan didn't know too much about the player who was eventually to inherit his famous number seven shirt. Indeed he was on the same plane from Heathrow Airport as Tyneside-born Peter Beardsley, on his way to complete his £250,000 signing from Vancouver Whitecaps. The Geordie was too shy to introduce

29

himself to one of his role models and as for Keegan, he didn't even recognise a player who was to become an integral cog in United's promotion charge in the months ahead.

It didn't take too long for Keegan to wax lyrical over the newcomer. Indeed Beardsley's dazzling display in a riveting 5–0 victory over fierce rivals Manchester City on 29 October 1983 is still talked about in pubs to this very day. The former Carlisle forward, who'd spent an ill-fated spell at Manchester United, made his debut as a substitute at Barnsley and opened his Newcastle goals account in a 2–0 win against Cardiff at Ninian Park, the club's fourth successive league win. But against City, Toon fans witnessed a performance from the little maestro which fully vindicated Cox's decision to reshuffle his pack. Waddle was already beginning to fulfil his rich potential and the triumvirate of the former sausage factory worker, Keegan and the newcomer proved far too potent for shell-shocked City. Beardsley grabbed a marvellous hat-trick and his two fellow strikers a goal apiece as Newcastle played with a passion and verve not seen for years. Such was their superiority that afternoon, I swear the man of the match was City goalkeeper Alec Williams. But for him, United could have hit double figures.

Seven days later, Newcastle came back from the dead to beat Fulham 3–2 on home soil with Wharton grabbing a last-gasp winner. Watching from the stands was Keegan's former Liverpool manager Bob Paisley. Afterwards, he delivered his verdict on the team now handily placed in second spot: 'Kevin Keegan is Newcastle United, in fact they should rename them Keegan United,' he maintained. 'Everything goes through Kevin. He took throw-ins, free-kicks and doubled up as a striker and midfielder. He had more touches than the rest put together. His influence is unbelievable. He's playing as well as I've ever seen him at an age when most players are looking for a less demanding stint.'

As it happens, I disagreed with Paisley's assessment of United. In Waddle and Beardsley, United possessed two gifted individuals who won as many matches as Keegan that year. Midfield terrier McCreery was a revelation while at the back Anderson and Wharton were arguably the most underestimated full-backs in Division Two. But Paisley had a point. Such was the respect his team-mates had for Keegan, his very presence drove them on to greater heights. And rarely have I seen a player assume such responsibility on the pitch. Whether it was in defence or in the opposition area, he was always there ready to help out a team-mate. For all the strengths elsewhere in the side, rarely was a goal scored which didn't involve the skipper.

At the halfway stage, Keegan had scored 13 goals in 21 outings and Newcastle looked a good bet for a return to the top flight for the first time since 1978. Their hand was strengthened still further when Cox signed Glenn Roeder from Queen's Park Rangers. With Jeff Clarke sidelined for several months, the likeable Londoner was to prove an inspirational recruit as United's defence tightened up significantly following his arrival.

Newcastle went into the New Year full of optimism with a brace by Keegan securing a 2–1 win at Boundary Park on 31 December. Fans were quite naturally allowing their imaginations to run away with them wondering just what impact United's free-scoring forward line would have on the First Division come August. Keegan was as fit as a footballer ten years his junior, in the richest goal-scoring form of his career and almost overflowed with enthusiasm for the game he graced and loved. The future looked full of possibilities for United – and their leader.

But Newcastle and all their supporters were rocked when Keegan suddenly and unexpectedly announced his retirement at the end of that season. In view of subsequent events, I suppose we shouldn't have been so stunned. Here was someone who acted on his own instincts and rarely allowed outside opinion to temper his views. But when he called a press conference on St Valentine's Day – his 33rd birthday – the football world was shocked that someone who still had so much to offer as a player was quitting. To most of us, Keegan was as good as ever but the perfectionist himself disagreed. He took us back to an FA Cup tie at Liverpool a few weeks earlier to explain just why he was hanging up his boots.

I remember that Liverpool v Newcastle game for one reason above all others – the magnificent United supporters, 13,000 of whom took over Anfield that Friday night for a game being beamed out live on BBC television. United had gone into the game full of confidence despite the Reds' array of talent but, quite frankly, they were outclassed, losing 4–0 – and it could have been more. Keegan didn't play well but neither did any of his team-mates who seemed to freeze on the big stage. But the incident which provoked his decision to quit football spoke volumes for the standards he had set himself. Chasing a long ball, the Newcastle skipper was favourite to latch on to it until Mark Lawrenson, a magnificent defender at the peak of his powers, ate up the ground to dispossess his opponent. As far as KK was concerned, that was personal humiliation. In his opinion, such an incident would not have happened unless he was on the way down.

At 33, Keegan was not exactly old for a footballer but the prospect of winding down held no appeal at all. Promotion was now an obsession for a man determined to finish on a high. Indeed, United churned out the points with only a few scares along the way. They were at their scintillating best in beating Portsmouth 4–1 at Fratton Park. A shock 1–0 home defeat at the hands of promotion dark horses Grimsby was quickly followed by arguably the result of the season – a 2–1 victory over Manchester City in front of a 41,767 crowd at Maine Road. Keegan's performance that day was so inspiring. I remember writing an article in the *Evening Chronicle* urging Cox and his team-mates to persuade him to reconsider his decision to retire. I should have known better – his mind was made up.

By April, Chelsea and Sheffield Wednesday looked certain to fill the top two places in the Second Division with Newcastle holding a four-point lead over Manchester City in third spot. A 3–1 win at Charlton proved to be Keegan's last-ever game in the capital and the friendly hosts acknowledged that fact with a presentation to him before the game. How ironic that 13 years later he would lead Newcastle for the last time as a manager in an FA Cup-tie also at The Valley!

It was at Gallowgate, however, that the promotion party was in full cry. North neighbours Carlisle, who were enjoying their best season for years, were powerless to prevent United running riot on Easter Monday with Keegan and Beardsley scoring two apiece, Waddle finding the net and, just for good measure, Kevin Carr saving a penalty. An inexplicable defeat at doomed Cambridge, who hadn't won a league game since October, kept the champagne on ice but nothing could stop the celebrations exploding into lift-off after a 4–0 rout of struggling Derby. Promotion wasn't mathematically certain but no one seemed to care as Keegan led his team-mates on a lap of honour. Appropriately, Beardsley (two), Waddle and Keegan all scored, with the skipper receiving lengthy treatment for concussion after bravely going in with Derby keeper Steve Cherry to head United into the lead. A king-size headache didn't prevent Keegan wearing a smile as wide as the River Tyne as he shook hands, signed autographs and organised an impromptu photo-call on the pitch. By the time he made his way down the tunnel, he must have had about 20 scarves wrapped around his neck.

That head injury meant Keegan missed his only game of the 1983–84 season when 17,000 Geordies converged on Leeds Road to see Newcastle hit back from an early two-goal deficit to secure a 2–2 draw through Beardsley and Mills. The point made First Division football certain – not that anyone had thought otherwise before kick-off.

So came the day when Keegan prepared for his last-ever competitive game. St James's Park was bathed in sunshine on 12 May for a contest against Brighton which wasn't so much a match as a ceremony. The tensions of previous weeks had been replaced by collective euphoria laced with sadness that one of England's greatest-ever players was bowing out. Keegan was always one for style and so it was almost predestined that this would be his 500th league appearance since his debut in 1968. And the man who'd marked his Newcastle debut with a goal against QPR rounded it all off in the best way possible. It was almost as if the Almighty Himself was determined this would be Keegan's day, for his 171st league goal was possibly the easiest he'd ever scored – a simple tap-in after Joe Corrigan had failed to hold Waddle's shot. The final goal of a truly memorable season was one of St James's Park's all-time classics. Beardsley had become the master of the spectacular but his strike to make it 3–1 to Newcastle topped them all. Latching on to Keegan's pass (slightly under-hit as Kevin would admit later), his trademark drag-back left Eric Young grounded, before he cheekily lobbed Corrigan – all six feet five inches of him – to his 20th goal since joining Newcastle. Keegan had helped himself to 28 but with

33

young pretenders Beardsley and Waddle scoring 38 between them, the future seemed in safe hands. It was almost a case of The King is Dead, Long Live the Princes.

The Toon Army had indulged themselves after those wins against Derby and Brighton but there was still time for a third party – and it would prove to be the most poignant of them all. His former club Liverpool had agreed to play a farewell friendly against Newcastle on 17 May for a game which would see Keegan pull on a black and white shirt for the last time. It was pure theatre that Thursday night with 36,722 packed into St James's to pay homage and say goodbye to their Messiah. The match finished 2-2 with the second half interrupted by a flurry of substitutions, but who cared?

If those previous laps of honour had been spontaneous demonstrations of emotion, what happened on the final whistle was pre-planned, stage-managed and, some might say, over the top. But football had never quite witnessed an exit like this. Keegan had arranged a party for family, friends and team-mates at the Gosforth Park Hotel that night but before the drinks could flow, it was time to bid farewell to his disciples. A helicopter hovered over the stadium as an emotional Keegan, now on his own, walked around the perimeter before hovering in front of the West Stand and picking out his wife and young children in the directors' box. Then the helicopter landed on the centre circle and with the crowd not knowing whether to laugh, cry or cheer, he ran towards its door, turning once to wave a last goodbye. It must have been a strange sight watching thousands of hardened Geordies peering up to the heavens with their arms raised until the aircraft became a blip. But then for the last two years, Newcastle United had reached for the skies. At the time no one would have guessed they would try and reach even higher under Kevin Keegan the manager.

# 3

## THE BEGINNING:
## 1991–92

ON 1 JANUARY 1992, Newcastle United was at the lowest point in its long history. The team had been beaten 4-0 at Southend United, and, as they say in the game, they were lucky to get nil. They were bottom of the old Second Division, heading into the Third Divsion and possibly into oblivion for the first time in their history. A mere 36 days later Kevin Keegan took over. The fairytale began.

Keegan's predecessor was Ossie Ardiles. A lovely little man, he managed a team as he played. Under the little Argentinian, United were a joy to watch. He brought the kids through. In one match at West Ham, United fielded their youngest-ever pair of full-backs in their history with Steve Watson and Robbie Elliott. But as fast as United scored, they leaked goals at the other end.

In one embarrassing defeat against Middlesbrough at St James's Park on Boxing Day 1991, Paul Wilkinson was able to run 60 yards without a United defender in sight and score the winner. The next home game against Charlton Athletic was an even bigger disaster. United were leading 3–1. They lost 4–3. An irate United fan shouted to the press box, 'Oliver! You brought Ardiles, now you can get rid of him.' Yet, it was still a hard decision for United to sack Ardiles – even though Newcastle only won eight out of their 41 league games in ten awful months.

United's next game was at Oxford on 1 February. It was as

cold a day as you can imagine. The game typified everything about United under Ardiles. They played well but lost 5–2, with keeper Tommy Wright dropping a huge clanger for one of the goals. After the game John Cairns, one of the Newcastle radio reporters, asked United director Douglas Hall about the Ardiles position. The now infamous reply came straight back, 'He's as safe as houses.'

It wasn't said in a press conference, but as the United directors squeezed along a narrow corridor on the way to the car park. Knowing Douglas as I do, I could tell by the glint in his eye that he was talking very much tongue in cheek, and I wasn't in favour of sending the news back to the North-East. But I was outvoted and the following day's story was Hall junior saying Ossie's job was safe. It wasn't, of course. On the Monday night there was a board meeting with Ardiles to discuss the situation.

It was never made public, but on the same night Chief Executive Freddie Fletcher met former skipper Glenn Roeder in Newcastle with a view to him working with the United defence. And it was Fletcher himself who came up with the name which was to transform the club – Kevin Keegan. There had been some talk a couple of months earlier about Keegan coming in and doing some promotional work. But, knowing how popular Keegan was, this was actually blocked by Ardiles.

However, there was no blocking Keegan's appointment as manager on Wednesday, 5 February 1992. Keegan had been out of football for all of the eight years since he quit as a Newcastle United player after leading them to promotion in 1984. He had covered the odd game assisting the commentator on live television. But being a manager of one of the most famous clubs in the country was a different matter. He had tired of playing golf in the Spanish sunshine of his adopted home in Marbella. Kevin Keegan was ready for a new challenge.

Obviously Newcastle were taking a gamble on Keegan. But these were times that bordered on desperation. It's history now of course, but Keegan was an inspired choice by Freddie Fletcher. I've said it before and I'll say it again – there probably wasn't another man in the world capable of rescuing Newcastle United.

The *Evening Chronicle* had received a tip-off about what was about to happen. But it was still some occasion as Keegan strode out to face the press at the Newcastle Breweries Visitors' Centre. Keegan hardly looked any different from the night he was whisked away by helicopter from St James's Park after his testimonial against Liverpool that balmy night in 1984.

He had been back to Tyneside only once to watch United play out a rather drab goalless draw with Blackburn Rovers in October 1991, and to take part in the Centenary Celebrations. I remember receiving my copy – my gratis press copy – of Paul Joannou's excellent *United, The First 100 Years* as a memento for my son Mark. Several United players volunteered to sign it for me, including prolific goal scorer Mick Quinn. But I wasn't having any of this. There were only two signatures I wanted on such a memorable publication: Ossie Ardiles – he signed Osvaldo Ardiles – because he was such a world-wide figure and Kevin Keegan. I wanted Keegan's signature because I felt he had done so much for the club as a player leading them out of the Second Division wilderness back in 1984. As he signed the book for me, neither of us suspected just what an impact he was to have in the future, as manager of Newcastle United.

Keegan had been asked to write the foreword in Paul Joannou's masterpiece, and in it Keegan talked about his hurt that his beloved United were playing outside the top flight again. He said he was particularly hurt because, despite his experiences playing for Liverpool, Hamburg and Southampton, Newcastle United had, without question, the most loyal fans in football, the best fans he ever played for. He wrote that the fans were United's best collateral, the reason why he would always have to be optimistic about the future at St James's Park, and that the Geordie supporters had a thread of optimism running through them that is unique in football. Keegan told the fans that the biggest compliment he could pay them was choosing to retire as a Newcastle player.

He could hardly have guessed that just over five years later he would also retire as Newcastle manager, and those who knew him best said he would never take charge of another football club in this country. His foreword for Joannou's book came straight from the heart. He said if he could make a wish for football in general it would be to have a successful Newcastle United, and that the fans got the team on the pitch that their loyalty deserved.

These were prophetic words from Keegan. And doubtless they were foremost in his mind as the television cameras whirred away when he shook hands with Sir John Hall and the rest of the United board at his inauguration.

When Keegan was in Spain in 1985, he had said that only one thing was certain: if anyone anywhere read that Kevin Keegan was coming back to football full-time, they could laugh as much as he would. He said that it would never happen. But here he was seven years later saying that managing Newcastle United was the only job in football he ever wanted. It was music to the ears of every Newcastle United supporter as the news of his appointment hit Tyneside.

After Keegan had been wheeled out to face the press at the Newcastle Breweries Visitors' Centre, the press all trooped off to Ossie's house in Jesmond. Ossie just sat there as the whole circus walked across his garden and the muck flew on to the whitest carpets I have ever seen. Funnily enough, Freddie Fletcher, who had been sent to sack Ardiles at his own home, was later to move into the very same house.

But Keegan had to get a much bigger house in order – at St James's Park. His only brief was to keep Newcastle United in the Second Division, and he only had 16 games to do it. His first call was to his old mate, Terry McDermott. Like Keegan, who had retired to Marbella after finishing his playing career with United in the promotion season of 1983–84, Terry Mac had been out of the game. But the pulling power of Keegan was soon in evidence. His first game in charge was against Bristol City. United won 3–0 and the crowd had jumped from the 15,663 of the previous home game against Charlton to 29,263.

Keegan was back with a bang. Back to the only job he would have returned to football for. But it wasn't all easy. In Keegan's own words, the club and the team were a shambles. Keegan was only prepared to commit himself until the end of the season. But after just 38 days and seven games in charge, Keegan and McDermott walked out.

It was the Friday before the Swindon match, Friday, 13 March. The United pair checked out of the Gosforth Park Hotel where they were both staying and set off for the tranquillity of the

Lake District. They only got as far as the Haydon Bridge before Keegan turned the car round and went back to the North-East. True to form, Keegan said nothing to his players, but guided them to a 3–1 win over an unsuspecting Swindon. Then on the final whistle Keegan was off again. This time he did not stop until he got to the family home he had retained in Romsey. Terry McDermott headed back to his native Liverpool.

The telephone wires were hot on the Sunday between Sir John Hall's Wynyard Hall home and Keegan in Hampshire. Keegan's beef was that money which had been promised from the board had not been forthcoming. He came out with a phrase that was to become a famous quote, 'It wasn't like it said in the brochure.' The first Keegan crisis was averted when Sir John and Lady Hall lodged a personal cheque at the club. However, there is no doubt in my mind that on that Monday Keegan returned to Tyneside, the ground rules had been laid. Kevin Keegan was now bigger than the club. It was a situation which was to remain until Keegan's shock resignation just under five years later. That cheque lodged by Sir John and Lady Hall was to give Keegan the player he believed did more than anyone to keep United in the Second Division – Brian Kilcline. In my view, Keegan was badly advised in his early transfer dealings.

Two of his first three buys, Darren McDonough and Peter Garland, did not work out. But the other man, dubbed Killer, was a huge success. He cost £250,000 from Oldham, and Keegan even got £100,00 back for him when he sold him to Swindon nearly two years later.

Keegan knew that Killer was an awesome sight on the field with his flowing locks and moustache. But off the field Killer was a gentleman, apart from when he was on the wrong end of the practical jokes that are part and parcel of all football clubs these days. Nobody ever owned up when Killer fell asleep in the Cyprus sun, on the club's end-of-season relaxation trip, and woke up to find that all of his hair had been cut off. Nobody dared.

Of all the players' columns I have done in 17 years covering United, Killer was the only one who thanked me with a Christmas bottle of whisky – a small one, mind you – until Les Ferdinand paid for a United shirt for my daughter Suzanne last year. And on the day when Keegan quit, the phone rang and a gentle voice asked, 'Have you drunk that whisky yet?' I knew who it was. Killer. Brian Kilcline was the only one of his former players to contact me on the day Keegan resigned. The United players took their inspiration from Killer as they set about trying to stave off the relegation which would have put the very future of the club in jeopardy.

However, it was never going to be easy. Things were tense, but there were lighter moments. It's usual practice for the press to seek out any United match-winner after the game. But when Steve Watson grabbed the only goal of the game at Port Vale, we found that the teenager was waiting for us by the time we clambered down the gantry from the press box and into our press room.

Keegan inspired United to a little run. They beat Cambridge and Swindon, drew at Grimsby, and then beat derby rivals Sunderland with a David Kelly goal. But two days later Keegan took his side to Molineux, where United were on the wrong end of a 6–2 drubbing by Wolves. This was the first of five defeats on the trot, and United had a disastrous day at Derby County on the Easter Monday. Not only did they lose, they had three men, Kevin Scott, Kevin Brock and Liam O'Brien, sent off. Terry McDermott was also cautioned. Keegan and his great pal, the then Derby manager Arthur Cox, were seen to be having words on the touchline. For the first time it looked as though Keegan was going to fail.

To make matters worse, Keegan was charged with misconduct by the Football Association, along with Terry Mac who had been ordered out of the dug-out by referee Brian Coddington. Keegan's charge came completely out of the blue, but the United manager admitted that he had passed a comment to Coddington and that it had not been a surprise to him that he had been reported. When the case was heard just before the start of the following season Keegan was fined £1,000 and warned about his future conduct. Terry Mac received a similar warning as well as a £250 fine. Funnily enough Blackburn boss Kenny Dalglish – later to replace Keegan at St James's Park – was also warned about his future conduct at the same disciplinary hearing.

The day after the Derby defeat, I looked for the first time at just which teams United would be facing in the Third Division if they went down. But United had one last chance, as long as they beat Portsmouth in their final home game of the season. I'm glad to say I played a little part. I had become particularly friendly with Ray Ranson in his days as Newcastle right-back. Just before the transfer deadline Keegan had agreed to let Ranson join Reading. Ranson wasn't sure what to do and asked my advice. I told him he was too good to go down among the dead men in the lower division. He stayed and it was Ranson who clipped a superb ball forward for Mick Quinn who nudged it into the path of Kelly for a late winner against Portsmouth. It was probably the most important goal in United's history. Tyneside breathed a huge and collective sigh of relief. Keegan could still do it.

Leicester at Filbert Street was United's last game of the 1991–92 season. Victory would keep United up no matter what the other relegation candidates did. It was to prove to be an unbelievable, emotion-packed day for Keegan. The tension eased only slightly when Gavin Peacock gave United the lead with a scrambled goal just before half-time, a lead they were to hold until the final minute. Then Leicester, who were trying to win promotion, equalised through their war horse, Steve Walsh.

The United players were dazed. Were they relegated? Amazingly, the question was answered by Steve Walsh who turned the ball into his own net in injury time to give United one of the most dramatic wins in their history. Keegan had done it. Or had he? The Leicester fans invaded the pitch and when David Elleray took the players off the field nobody knew if the game was over or not.

Even Keegan did not know whether he had done the job he had been asked to do. Then David Elleray finally confirmed that the match was over and United had won. Kevin Keegan, the man who has never failed at anything in his life, *had* done it again. He had kept Newcastle United in the Second Division, and probably in existence. But he always said he could break out in a cold sweat when he remembers how close United came to being relegated.

Typically, he was not interested in personal glory. He was more concerned that Newcastle United must never get in this position again. While Keegan had done the job, nothing had been decided about the future. But as the ecstatic Geordies made their way back up the M1 that Saturday night, there wasn't one United fan who did not believe Keegan would be at the helm again in the following season. Nor was there a Newcastle United fan who could have guessed that Leicester City again would provide the last-day opposition in exactly 12 months time, and that the result would reverberate around football. In the meantime, they were just happy that one job had been done. A new era was about to begin as Keegan set his sights on bringing United some success.

# 4

## SUCCESS AT LAST:
## 1992–93

THERE SHOULD NOT have been cause for so much optimism at the start of 1992–93. But there was. After all, United had only been one game away from relegation to the old Third Division and possible oblivion a couple of months earlier.

The mood was most definitely upbeat for two reasons. First, Kevin Keegan who had only taken the manager's post until the end of the previous season had agreed to come back and finish the job. Second, Sir John Hall and his new board, including his son Douglas and Freddie Shepherd as Vice-Chairman, had finally won control of the club. The fight for control had been long, bitter at times and full of political intrigue. But the new board was full of ideas and it wasn't frightened to have a go at anything it felt would benefit Newcastle United.

It seemed hard to believe that only the previous November, Sir John, on a world cruise which was filmed by Alan Whicker for his *Whicker's World*, received a message to ring Douglas as he had dinner in Hong Kong. United were in danger of going out of existence and Sir John only had a couple of hours to save it. Eventually the United Chairman agreed to come up with the £680,000 needed to stop Newcastle United from going out of business.

All this seemed a million miles away as the United trio of Douglas Hall, Freddie Shepherd and Chief Executive Freddie

Fletcher jetted out of Newcastle and down to Marbella confident they would persuade Keegan to come back. The United deputation met Kevin and his wife Jean at a hotel while the Keegans' two girls splashed around in the pool. True to form, Keegan asked for and was given certain guarantees. He wanted to know where the club was going under the new regime and he was more than happy with what he heard. Keegan agreed a three-year deal with Terry McDermott as his assistant. Keegan had actually been paying Terry out of his own pocket, but on this occasion his trusty number two got a deal of his own.

But this wasn't all. A new adventurous United had been born under Keegan and the Halls. Chris Waddle's name had come up during the discussions and it was agreed all round that the former United favourite was just what was needed to get things going on the field in the new season. So instead of jetting home, the United party headed North-East to Marseilles and met The Waddler at his home in Aix-en-Provence. Waddle was as big as they come in France with Marseilles. But yes, he was interested in coming home.

It never happened, for a variety of reasons. But United were back in the big time and, most important of all, Keegan was back. He was left to manage the club the way he wanted. If in the next four years he wanted the grass at St James's Park to be pink, it would be pink the very next day.

Those tickled pink were the United fans, as Keegan cheekily picked up Paul Bracewell from derby rivals Sunderland. Brace had just skippered Sunderland at Wembley and after losing his third FA Cup final he moved on to St James's Park. John Beresford had been even unluckier. He had missed his effort in a penalty shoot-out with Liverpool in the replayed FA Cup semi-final and Portsmouth and Jim Smith were out. Yet Graeme Souness had seen enough of Beresford to try and sign him for Liverpool. Bez got as far as sitting in Souness's office at Anfield before the deal was called off, because of a supposedly 'dodgy' ankle. But Keegan was already beginning to show that he was very much his own man. He wasn't in the least put off by talk of a suspect ankle and Beresford followed Bracewell through the door in a £650,000 deal. Keegan wasn't finished.

He went to Souness and persuaded the Liverpool manager to let him have the versatile Barry Venison for a bargain £250,000.

Keegan was ready. So too were United. And the fans. Southend were not exactly the most attractive opposition to start the 1992–93 season at St James's Park, nevertheless United boasted the biggest attendance of the day in England – 28,545 – as the ball started rolling. No wonder there were huge smiles on the faces of the directors as United ran out 3–2 winners. Those smiles became bigger as Paul Bracewell paid back a fair portion of his £250,000 fee with the opening goal of the campaign. United were on their way.

In fact United got off to a real flyer, leaving their rivals in the starting blocks. Not surprisingly the fans, starved of success, turned up in droves. Amazingly 5,000 fans were locked out for the 3–1 win over Portsmouth. It was hard to believe that when Portsmouth were last in town a couple of months earlier, had United lost, they would probably have been relegated to the old Third Division and the whole future of the club would have been in doubt. Significantly United went to the top of the First Division after beating Pompey – and they stayed there until the end of the season.

By the time Bristol City arrived at St James's Park on 19 September, United had won seven out of seven league games and they had opened up a three-point gap at the top of the table. Bristol City of course had been Keegan's first managerial opponents seven months earlier when he at first named a ten-man team but on this occasion he managed to name a full side.

Keegan was already beginning to find out that he had entered a cut-throat business, for Jimmy Lumsden, the first manager he had pitted his wits against, had been sacked soon afterwards and it was Denis Smith who led Bristol City up the steps and into St James's Park. By now City had a young striker by the name of Andy Cole from Arsenal but he wasn't involved on this occasion. It's a good bet that Cole was pleased he wasn't as Bristol City were sent packing 5–0.

Yet Keegan still wasn't satisfied. He was made aware of a young player at Charlton Athletic, possibly by Keith Peacock, reserve team coach with the south London side and father of his own striker Gavin Peacock. The only problem was that the home-loving Cockney lad Robert Lee had already turned down former Charlton manager Lenny Lawrence at Middlesbrough because it was too far from home. But then the silver-tongued Keegan set about convincing Lee and his wife Anna that it was far easier getting to London from Newcastle than it was from Middlesbrough. He told Lee that he would have to get a taxi from Middlesbrough to Darlington and even then all the London-bound trains did not stop there while he could zip straight through from Newcastle to King's Cross. In the end Keegan must have worn Lee down. The result was that Lee joined United for £700,000 and he is undoubtedly a leading candidate as his best buy.

Robert Lee had just time to settle in as United equalled a record of 11 wins out 11 games when they went to Roker Park and won 2–1. Keegan, in fact, became the first United manager to win on Wearside since 1956. United had set a record of six consecutive away league victories and a record of 15 successive away league games without failing to score. To tell the truth, United started breaking so many records that even their keenest statistician lost track. But nobody could ever lose track of that Liam O'Brien free-kick which gave United victory at Roker Park.

Now only little Grimsby stood in the way of a record-breaking 12 wins in a row, and they had to come to St James's Park. Grimsby had trouble finding a goalkeeper and in the end they brought in former United man Dave Beasant. The visitors were expected to be lambs to the slaughter. But someone forgot to tell them. When Jim Dobbin gave them a last-minute victory, Keegan took it on the chin. But Grimsby had won fair and square. They hadn't tried to kick United off the park and referee Paul Harrison did not have to make any controversial decisions. Little were United to realise what significance Grimsby were to play in their season, but the result kept everyone's feet on the ground.

United's only aim was promotion. There was no gnashing of teeth when Chelsea knocked them out of the Coca-Cola Cup, especially as United had beaten Middlesbrough at Ayresome Park in the previous round. It was this result perhaps more than any other which made me realise United were back in the big time. It wasn't only the fact that United were picking up the points, it was the way Keegan had them doing it which caught the imagination of the whole country.

However, late in October and early November, United hit a problem with the defeat against Grimsby being followed by the Coca-Cola Cup exit at Chelsea and another League reverse at Leicester.

They got back into the swing of things again with a real battling 3–2 victory at Birmingham City. United even won despite playing without a regular keeper for the whole of the second half. Tommy Wright was actually injured in the opening minutes but soldiered on until half-time when United led 3–2. Midfielder Kevin Brock went in goal for the second half and amazingly managed to keep a clean sheet as United moved nine points clear of Swindon at the top of the First Division table.

The joy was tempered with the news the following day that former Chairman Stan Seymour had died overnight in his Birmingham hotel. Kevin Keegan was particularly saddened by the passing of 'young' Stan, son of another former United Chairman of the same name. Seymour junior had been Chairman when Keegan had first arrived at St James's Park in the summer of 1982 and there was a bond between the two men. 'Young' Stan was a larger than life character and even though he was a part of the old regime, the new board kept him involved as Vice-President.

United could have done without any distractions in their quest for a place into the money-spinning Premiership, but they had one in the Anglo-Italian Cup. Entry was compulsory and even United attracted poor gates for their home games – 9,789 for Ascoli, and 4,609 against Cesena. The only excitement in the first match was when Ascoli coach Cacciatori was restrained by Keegan.

But the disappointing attendances were nothing to the crowds in Italy. There were only 744 for the game in Lucchese – the lowest for a game in United's history – and most of those were United supporters. And a measly 1,229 were spread around Bari's vast and magnificent 60,000-seater stadium – the Stadia

San Nicola which was developed especially for the 1990 World Cup.

Fortunately for United they went out of the competition at the first hurdle, but Keegan had cleverly marshalled his troops. Those players not winning a regular place in the league side like Brian Kilcline, Franz Carr, Alan Thompson and Mattie Appleby were given valuable games. This helped to keep the fringe players happy, but after returning from Lucchese Keegan put Carr, Kevin Brock, Appleby and Mick Quinn on the transfer list.

Keegan wanted United to do well on the weekend of the club's 100th birthday. They did, winning 2–0 at Notts County to ease themselves 12 points clear at the top of the table.

By the turn of the year things were going so well that Keegan volunteered the opinion that it was an easy job managing Newcastle United. He said that the players were a dream to handle and revealed that they were all putting in extra work after the normal training sessions. Even at this stage he said the fact that United were now playing in front of sell-out crowds at St James's Park would be a big benefit next season when the club was in the Premier League. Not *if* the club was in the Premier League, but *when*. Keegan's confidence in them must have been a tremendous boost to the United players.

He reflected on 1992 picking out two games which stood out – that last-gasp end-of-season win at Leicester and another victory at Peterborough.

Peterborough was an amazing day. The September sun beat down mercilessly on the United fans at London Road, and there were certainly plenty of them – an estimated 7,000 in a crowd of 14,487. In fact it was touch and go whether there were more United supporters than home fans. Keegan looked at the support and said to himself that with all this United could take on and beat the world.

United took the town over in their first league visit to this little part of Cambridgeshire. Chairman Sir John Hall and Lady Mae, Douglas Hall and Freddie Shepherd travelled to Peterborough by train. They were fêted every mile of the way by the happy United fans. And yes, United won by Kevin Sheedy's goal on the hour to make it seven out of seven. Talk about being in seventh heaven.

The New Year arrived with United still 12 points clear of Tranmere. Keegan then led United to their biggest third-round FA Cup victory since 1974 with four goals in the second half in a 4–0 St James's Park win over Port Vale. Keegan admitted he had spoken hard words to his side at half-time, reminding his players that they had not achieved things by just going through the motions. There were also words between Keegan and Mick Quinn. Quinn, sold to Coventry, started it all with a vitriolic attack on Keegan accusing him of 'hypocrisy'. Keegan perhaps would have done better to ignore his former player, but in turn he branded Quinn 'a Judas'.

Back on the pitch Keegan's words continue to inspire United. On 9 January United beat a Bristol City side which included a certain Andrew Cole. While delighted at his own side for winning a game 'we would have lost a year ago', Keegan noted the performance of young Cole.

Nothing could stop Keegan or United. Not even the Government. Unbelievably United's game at Southend was brought forward to 20 January because of the Young Conservatives conference in the Essex seaside town on the February date of the scheduled fixture. It meant an extra midweek game. Despite the presence of an up-and-coming striker by the name of Stan Collymore in the Southend side, United picked up a 1–1 draw and moved 15 points clear at the top of the table – their biggest-ever lead of the season.

On 5 February Keegan celebrated one year as manager of Newcastle United. He had had a real crash course in football management. He joked at the time: 'If they taught it at university they would set up a simulated course like I have had and people would say it's too far-fetched. But it's actually happened and I still believe it's only the start.'

Yes, it was only the start, but things were certainly happening as suddenly everybody wanted to see Keegan's United. Rotherham got their first capacity gate for 22 years for their FA Cup fourth-round tie with United. Keegan celebrated his first year in charge by guiding United to a 2–0 win over Rotherham in the replay. Hadn't the first year flown by? Keegan took his squad to Marbella immediately after the game for a break as he kept his players in the best of condition.

Keegan himself was struck down by the flu bug and missed the fifth-round tie at Blackburn Rovers. So the much publicised Keegan v Kenny Dalglish face-to-face did not happen. Keegan, listening to the game on the radio back at Wynyard, must have suffered a relapse when Roy Wegerle got the only goal of the game in injury time.

Keegan was back for the crucial game at West Ham, eight days later. With United four points ahead of the Hammers it was important they did not lose. They didn't, grinding out a goalless draw.

Wednesday, 24 February, was a bad night all round. Bobby Moore, England's 1966 World Cup-winning captain and a big pal of Keegan, had died of cancer earlier in the day, plunging the whole country into mourning. United then proceeded to play out a goalless draw with Bristol Rovers – and probably for the first time Keegan heard his side booed off. He wasn't exactly happy but United's nerves were beginning to show.

Keegan picked United straight up with successive and impressive victories over Tranmere and Brentford. He was particularly pleased to come away from Prenton Park with the three points in a 3–0 win over Tranmere. Despite working on a shoestring budget Tranmere manager Johnny King had kept the Merseyside outfit in the promotion race. United had not scored in their previous four games – Bristol Rovers, West Ham, Blackburn Rovers and Portsmouth – and Keegan obviously did not want this to continue. Not only that but the game was being beamed out live by Sky Television. United had not done all that well in front of the live cameras and there was beginning to be talk of jinx – something Keegan hated. All this ended as United increased their lead at the top of the table to seven points.

So the nerves were quite calm by the time Brentford arrived at St James's Park at the beginning of March. United swarmed all over the Bees and hit five goals. But it was the goal which did not count that was the talking point on Tyneside that night. Even Keegan who must have thought he had seen it all before was baffled by it all. United were coasting at 4–1 when Brentford keeper Graham Benstead raced 30 yards out of his goal and, as Alan Neilson closed in, booted the ball back into the Newcastle half. The ball went to Robert Lee who quickly weighed up the situation. Lee brought the ball down and from over 60 yards dispatched it straight back over the head of the stranded Benstead and into the back of the empty net.

Lee, the United team on the field, the United management team off it and the supporters went wild. But amid all the celebrations Preston referee Ian Hendrick had given United a free-kick just inside their half. His linesman had flagged offside against one of the Brentford front men when Benstead had first kicked the ball forward. So probably for the first time in the history of the game a team had had a goal disallowed for offside against the opposing team. There was certainly never a dull moment under Keegan's United. But he was still not prepared to take any chances. He bought Scott Sellars and Mark Robinson from Leeds and Barnsley respectively at a combined cost of just over £1 million.

The big one was yet to come, and he came in just before the transfer deadline for £1.75 million from Bristol City. Andy Cole got his first goal for United in his full debut against his home town team Notts County. Keegan said: 'It was a real striker's goal. He will get a few more of them.' Too true, Kevin.

When Keegan flew his squad down to Stansted for the game at Cambridge, United won 3–0, the 11th win on their travels, to equal a club record which had stood since 1936–37. Then Keegan purred in delight as United trounced Barnsley 6–0, the first victory by such a margin since 1964. All this was nothing to the delight of the United fans when they beat Sunderland 1–0 at St James's Park to record the double over their Wearside rivals. To be perfectly honest, the game should never have been played after a torrential downpour on the morning of the match. But the game was being beamed out by Sky and there was no date for United to fix up another game had Sheffield referee Keith Hackett given the thumbs-down. It was Scott Sellars who got the thumbs-up from the United fans when his tenth minute free-kick was bent over the visiting wall and against Tony Norman's post before going into the net for the only goal.

United were in heaven. The only disappointment for their fans was that they had not secured promotion against their deadliest rivals. However, only two more points were needed and United had three games in which to get them. Grimsby was the next port of call.

How United took over the fishing town that night. But at the back of the mind of every United fan was that Grimsby victory – the only one in the league – at St James's Park earlier in the season. Perhaps that's why the United supporters spilled over on to the pitch in their excitement when Andy Cole opened the scoring just after the break, causing a six-minute hold-up. But this was nothing to the scenes when David Kelly wrapped things up in the time added on for that stoppage. Kelly himself was so excited that he tipped the physio's bucket of cold water over Keegan. Even hard-bitten journalists like myself were affected.

I gladly put my hand in my pocket and bought a round of drinks. It's the only time I've seen Terry McDermott with a glass in his hand since he came back. Once Keegan had dried out following his soaking, he remained calm but he must have been bubbling over inside. His decision to come back had been vindicated.

There was yet time for United to put in a terrible performance but still beat Oxford two days later as Keegan went home at half-time still suffering from that persistent flu bug.

Then came Leicester – yes, the same Leicester that United had played in such different circumstances in the last match 12 months earlier – in the final game of the season. And the carnival. Fittingly it was at St James's Park. Brian Kilcline and Barry Venison were presented with the Championship trophies before the game. The result did not appear to matter, but anyone who thought this does not know Kevin Keegan. Keegan said later he wanted to finish with a bang.

Yet even he could not have envisaged what was to come. He later described it as perfection. United were six up at half-time – the first time they had scored six in one half since 1946. United ended up winning 7–1 with both Andy Cole and David Kelly helping themselves to hat-tricks – the first time two United players had scored three in the same match again since 1946.

With a couple of minutes to go to half-time, Keegan stood with Terry McDermott looking around the ground. The whole place was a sea of black and white. Keegan could not hear himself speak for the noise. The warning had gone out to the rest of the teams in the Premiership. Kevin Keegan and Newcastle United were on their way.

# 5

# THE DEAL THAT SHOOK SOCCER: ANDY COLE

If Kevin Keegan had two big qualities as a manager, they were honesty and bravery. Well, Keegan certainly had to be brave to sell Andy Cole, and even braver to go out and face the fans on the steps of St James's Park when the news spread like wildfire, not only around Tyneside but the whole of the country. Yet, perhaps the bravest decision of all was to buy Cole in the first place. George Graham had allowed Cole to leave Arsenal and link up with Bristol City. Some said it was because he had an attitude problem. The vibes were not good about him. But Kevin Keegan has always judged a footballer on what he could do on the field. He was never afraid of reputations. He knew that any player coming to St James's Park would respect him so much that they would toe the line.

Funnily enough though, there was to be a big and very public bust-up between Cole and Keegan later. When United had played Bristol City at Ashton Gate in the January of 1993, Cole did not catch the ordinary eye. Indeed, Sir John Hall was to say that he had not seen anything that day to make him think Cole was worth buying. I cannot recall Cole making any sort of impression on me that day. Yes, Cole played his part as Wayne Allison gave Bristol City an early lead before United started the long trek home, 2–1 winners thanks to goals from David Kelly and Kevin Scott. Certainly Kevin Keegan and Terry McDermott had seen enough.

In fact, one incident when Cole took on and beat Steve Howey, one of the fastest men on United's books for pace, made him special in the eyes of Keegan. Cole was never far from Keegan's mind over the next couple of months as the United manager sought the one big signing which would guarantee the Championship.

With Bristol being in the West Country and Keegan not having a lot of time to go scouting, it was obviously difficult to check on Cole. Yet one night Keegan and Terry McDermott noticed that Bristol City and Cole were playing West Ham. The kick-off was quarter to eight. It was just before five in the afternoon. By a quirk of fate, United Director Douglas Hall popped his head into Keegan's office. Within minutes the United contingent were on their way to the airport and heading west in Cameron Hall's private jet to Bristol.

Unknown to Keegan, Cole was actually doubtful for the game with an injury. What a waste of time and money this could have been. But Cole played, despite not being 100 per cent fit. This itself showed Keegan that Cole had plenty of guts and that he was prepared to put the team before himself. Keegan made up his mind. He wanted Cole. United put their bid in, but every time it was turned down. The main problem was that Arsenal manager George Graham had been wise enough to put in a sell-on clause if ever Cole were to move on from Bristol City. So one-third of any transfer fee in the empty Bristol City coffers would find its way back to Highbury.

Keegan brought in other players. A week before the transfer deadline on Tuesday, 9 March, Mark Robinson and Scott Sellars arrived from Barnsley and Leeds respectively for £450,000 and £700,000. But Cole was still the big fish Keegan wanted to haul in. Keegan happened to mention this to Douglas Hall and Sir John over lunch on the Thursday. This was all the Halls needed. They were galvanised into action without even telling Keegan.

The fact that United had such a small board meant that quick decisions were able to be made. The committee for buying players was Keegan, Douglas Hall, Vice-Chairman Freddie Shepherd and Chief Executive Freddie Fletcher before everything was put in front of Sir John Hall. But Bristol City ran a different sort of ship. United raised the £1.75 million with the help of Club President Trevor Bennett and strip sponsors Asics, and the Halls came up with the remainder.

That would have seemed to be the hardest part. But it wasn't. The hardest part was down at Bristol where all of their 13 directors had to give any transfers their individual approval. But United had a stroke of luck. The City board had a meeting at tea-time. United were in no mood for messing about. They told their Bristol counterparts that they had five minutes to make up their minds or the money would be spent elsewhere.

This ultimatum worked. United could have Andy Cole. The next job was to find the player. His car was discovered in the centre of Bristol and a note left on the windscreen telling him to contact his chairman urgently. And where else would the bachelor boy be on a Thursday night? In his local laundry, of course.

Keegan was delighted at the acquisition of Cole. The £1.75 million signing was unveiled to the press on the Friday lunch-time. The United team were already on the way to Swindon for the match the following day. Keegan and Cole followed later, ferried down by Sir John's chauffeur. The three North-East press lads who travelled all the time with United also motored down to Swindon. Both parties arrived at the same time and checked in at the reception in the Holiday Inn together. Lee Clark came bounding out of the restaurant to greet Cole, his England under-21 colleague.

But it was Keegan who was the most upbeat. As usual, the *Evening Chronicle* carried the Cole signing story first out of all the newspapers, but because of the timing of it, we had missed the first of our seven editions. It was that first edition which had travelled down to Swindon and which Keegan had seen. So over pre-dinner drinks – mine not his – he taunted me, 'Alan, do the *Chronicle* know that the *Titanic* has sunk?' The rest of the United party almost spilled their drinks with laughter. And how many times did Andy Cole peel away with a huge grin on his face after scoring for Newcastle United? Well, it was 68. In just 84 starts, in 22 months at the club.

Keegan left him on the bench for the first 63 minutes that day at Swindon, but seven days later he made a scoring full debut against Notts County and did not stop scoring until just before his sensational £7 million move to Manchester United. There had been the odd problem, especially Cole's runner which saw him miss the Coca-Cola League Cup defeat at Wimbledon, at the end of October in the first season back in the Premiership. Then there was the stress fracture which saw him dramatically taken out of a huge chunk of his last season. At the time he was experiencing his first goal drought since arriving at St James's Park. Indeed in his nine games before he was sold, Cole had failed to score. But like Keegan, Cole was a god on Tyneside. His record 41 league goals in one season for United may stand forever unless Alan Shearer beats it.

So if ever a transfer deal came out of the blue then Cole's move to Manchester United did. It was a bombshell, not only to the fans up and down the country but to the United directors. They were actually looking for someone to play alongside Cole. They had made a secret bid for Les Ferdinand, but Queen's Park Rangers feared a backlash from their fans and said no. Keegan was also interested in the Newcastle-born Chris Armstrong who was then at Crystal Palace, but again the answer was no. Alex Ferguson must have expected a similar response when he asked Keegan about Cole. Keegan had made the first move making an inquiry for Manchester United's Keith Gillespie. Ferguson countered, 'What about Andy Cole?' The very idea of letting Cole go shocked Keegan, just as much as it did the thousands of Newcastle United fans later.

Most of Keegan's discussions, transfers or otherwise, took place in a little office at the club's training ground at Durham. It was where the players were given their rockets by Keegan and his staff. Yet it was no bigger than a little cubby-hole. I should know. It was where Keegan sent me to face the wrath of Paul Bracewell when I dared to suggest that he might be joining Sunderland – a couple of weeks before he actually did.

The Sunday before Cole was sold, United had a home FA Cup-tie with Blackburn Rovers at St James's Park, and it was training as usual at Durham the day before. I was actually interviewing Pavel Srnicek for a feature after training and I thought we were the only two left at the training ground.

Suddenly, the door to the little office opened and out walked Keegan. I was a bit surprised to find he was still there, but thought nothing of it. I realised later that Keegan had probably been holding discussions with Ferguson on a transfer which would shake the world, less than 20 yards from where I was sitting. What if I had overheard Keegan discussing the Cole deal with Ferguson? I'm glad that I didn't.

Keegan's first job was to convince his directors that he should sell Cole and bring in Gillespie. He met Vice-Chairman Freddie Shepherd and together they headed for Douglas Hall's home. Douglas had hardly had the time to let them in when Keegan, never one to beat about the bush, hit him with the possibility of Cole going.

Publicly, the transfer was put at a £7 million package. Cole was valued at £6 million and Gillespie at £1 million. But Keegan's own valuation of Gillespie was £2.5 million. That meant Cole was worth £8.5 million to Newcastle United if the deal went through. Keegan told the United hierarchy that the more he thought about the deal the more he thought it was right for Newcastle.

The United directors had never failed to back Keegan, and they did again. While all this was going on, Cole, who was unaware of the situation, played for United in the draw with Blackburn on the Sunday. Once again he drew a blank. Robert Lee got the United equaliser in the 1–1 draw. On the Monday, Manchester United were playing Sheffield United in their FA Cup-tie at Bramall Lane. Keegan and the two Freddies, Shepherd and Fletcher, motored down to Sheffield. They met Sir John Hall down there. As usual, once he got over the initial surprise about the proposed Cole deal, the chairman backed his manager.

On the journey down, Keegan phoned Cole on the car phone A shocked Cole made it clear to Keegan he did not want to leave Newcastle, even for Manchester United. But Keegan convinced Cole it was a great chance for him, and he at least agreed to talk to Alex Ferguson. Ferguson wisely pulled Gillespie out of the FA Cup-tie, and all the parties, minus Cole, met in the Hallam Tower Hotel. When Gillespie realised Ferguson was happy for him to be a makeweight in the Cole deal, Keegan did not have much trouble in persuading the Northern Ireland youngster to find a peg in St James's Park.

Meanwhile, Cole and his agent Paul Stretford travelled through the night for an early breakfast with Ferguson, before agreeing the final part of the deal. Now the only job was informing the media so that they could let the world know. On the Tuesday morning Keegan had the opportunity to tell the press, but he decided against this. United's policy under Keegan concerning outgoing transfers was always to let the buying club make the announcement. I had watched the Manchester United game at Sheffield United on Sky Television. The cameras kept flashing on to the Newcastle contingent huddled together in the stands. There was nothing unusual in Keegan being there as Newcastle were playing Manchester United at St James's Park the following weekend. But one thing bugged me. The Newcastle party were still sitting there on the final whistle.

Now in normal circumstances when managers go on scouting trips they usually leave five or ten minutes before the end, to beat the traffic. But there they were on the final whistle. The whole Newcastle hierarchy. The red warning lights were flashing in my mind. I was actually on a day off the following day, but I was in the office working on one of our *Evening Chronicle* supplements. Still feeling a bit uneasy about it, I rang my counterpart on the *Manchester Evening News*, David Meek, to tell him to keep an eye on things. Sure enough, a couple of hours later the phone on my desk rang. It was one of David Meek's colleagues, Paul Hince. 'Ollie,' said Hincey, 'are you busy?' I said I wasn't. He quipped, 'Well, you are now. Manchester United have just bought Andy Cole for £7 million.'

My then Editor Neil Benson and Sports Editor Paul New were engaged in a conversation literally at my shoulder. What I said and the expression on my face stopped them in their tracks. It was big news, the biggest imaginable at the time. We slapped it right across both our front and back pages. As soon as the *Evening Chronicle* hit the streets, Newcastle was in a state of shock, equalled only two years later when Keegan himself quit.

The angry fans headed to St James's Park. They demanded to see Keegan. Not many managers would have faced them. Keegan did. Standing defiantly on the steps and in the full glare of the television cameras, he took on the supporters. Most were hostile. Keegan told them he understood how they felt. He told them that if he had got it wrong then he would pay the ultimate price by losing his job.

I couldn't help laughing at one supporter. He accused Keegan of selling his prize asset to United's biggest rivals, Manchester United. There was only one answer to that. Before Keegan returned to St James's Park, United's biggest rivals had been Grimsby Town. And Southend United. Another fan complained that it was just like the bad old days when Newcastle sold their best players, when stars like Chris Waddle, Peter Beardsley and Paul Gascoigne would develop at Newcastle only to go and shine most brightly in more distant skies. The fan confronted Keegan with a pledge made in the club's official board literature, that Newcastle were now a buying and not a selling club. Keegan tried to reassure him that new players would come but the fan said, 'Oh Kevin, we've seen it all before'. But they had seen nothing yet. Keegan would be true to his word. More than £60 million true to his word.

As usual, he came out with a quote that had the journalists drooling at the mouth. 'If I've got it wrong then there's a bullet with my name on it.' After the initial shock and anger, the vast majority of supporters backed Keegan. For what it's worth, at the time I thought Keegan was wrong to sell Andy Cole. Time has proved Keegan was right, yet again.

When the dust settled I could not help musing over my last dealing with Andy Cole. I had always got on well with him but, unfortunately, we did not part the best of friends. When I broke the news in the *Evening Chronicle* that he was going to become a father, Andy, a private man away from the glare of Newcastle United, was not amused.

On the Friday before his transfer, Andy confronted me. He told me that he had another three and a half years of his contract to run, and that during those three and a half years he would never give me another story. That was on the Friday lunchtime. By the Monday night he had gone.

# 6

## BACK WITH THE BIG BOYS: 1993–94

IT SEEMED AS though the summer would never end. The waiting was unbearable. And the anticipation was at fever pitch. Newcastle United were back in the big time. The memories of promotion and the civic reception had been fantastic. The United fans just could not wait for the new season to start.

It came out later that Kevin Keegan had not wanted to be in the parade as it wound its way through the city from the Gosforth Park Hotel down to Newcastle Civic Centre. Keegan wanted all the glory to go to the players but he was finally persuaded to change his mind by the United directors. Make no mistake, Keegan would already be thinking about the new season – even though 1992–93 had only just ended.

Keegan knew exactly who he wanted and what he had to do. The player he wanted most of all was Peter Beardsley: the same Beardsley who had played alongside him in the promotion season of 1983–84 and the man he always affectionately called Pedro because of the way he hauled the goals in.

There was one problem – Beardsley's age. Beardsley's birth certificate showed that he was 32. But Keegan knew better than anyone that Pedro still had so much to offer, and just as important, he knew what the top flight was all about after starring for both Liverpool and Everton after leaving United.

The Premiership was going to be new to so many of the United players like John Beresford, Andy Cole and Robert Lee and Keegan knew that Beardsley would give them instant credibility.

Yet lo and behold who else was trying to snap up Beardsley from Everton? None other than Derby boss Arthur Cox who had managed both Keegan and Beardsley in that earlier promotion season. But the United board, especially chairman Sir John Hall, remained sceptical of paying out £1.5 million because of the Geordie boy's age. Sir John stood his ground even though he said he knew Beardsley was a quality player. He insisted he was worried about paying over £1 million for a player who was over 30 and who would have no sell-on value. The chairman pointed out that he had also been against buying Roy Aitken because he was too old – and had been proved right. But Keegan was still adamant that he wanted Beardsley and he had yet to play his trump card. There was nothing for it but to tell the United board that their bitter rivals Sunderland had thrown their hat into the ring for the little striker. As Keegan later put it, it was a 'little fib'. But it worked.

I don't believe for one minute that Sir John really thought Sunderland had come in for Beardsley but it gave him a way out, and to his credit Sir John was quick to admit he was wrong about Beardsley. But there was still the problem of getting Beardsley's signature on to paper. Keegan was actually trying to pull off a double deal that summer's day in 1993 – Beardsley and Russian striker Sergei Yuran who had played for Benfica and Porto and who ended up on loan with Millwall.

Yuran was supposed to be first. But Keegan was not prepared to risk losing Beardsley. So with Terry Mac he travelled to a hotel at Wetherby and tied up the Beardsley deal. The England striker was so keen to return to St James's Park he was willing to take a drop in wages. Which is more than can be said about Yuran. Keegan and Terry Mac sped up to Teesside airport after sealing the Beardsley deal and flew to Heathrow where they met Yuran and his agents. But Keegan felt the vibes about Yuran were not right and he pulled out of the deal.

However, as the United pair headed back to the North-East they didn't care. They had got the one they really wanted. Peter Beardsley. Beardsley himself was delighted, saying that he always wanted to return home but never knew whether he was ever going to get the chance.

But two players who were not given their chance of a crack at the Premiership were strikers Gavin Peacock and David Kelly. Kelly had scored 28 goals in the promotion season and Peacock 18. Kelly, who was sold to Wolves for £750,000, was destined to be the subject of a quiz question for years to come. Which Newcastle United player scored a hat-trick on his last appearance for the club?

Peacock was a different case. His son had been born with part of his arm missing and Keegan let Peacock return to London and Chelsea for £1.25 million on compassionate grounds. Keegan also sold Andy Hunt, Alan Thompson and Mark Stimson to West Brom, Bolton Wanderers and Portsmouth respectively clawing another £450,000 into United's coffers. Once again he had shown he was not afraid to make decisions which might not be popular with the fans by selling Kelly and Peacock.

The board were prepared to match their manager in terms of bravery. For while Keegan had been reshaping his team the board were gradually rebuilding St James's Park. When the fans turned up for the opener against Spurs all but 1,000 of the 11,500 seats in the new North Stand – formerly the Leazes End – were filled. I had a sneak preview just after returning home from a holiday in Greece where quite naturally I marvelled at the Parthenon and Acropolis. When I told everyone that the new-look St James's Park had taken my breath away more than the wonders of ancient Athens I was ridiculed. But no one was laughing when the big day finally came.

The sun shone. The majority of the crowd proudly wore their black and white shirts. It was truly a magnificent setting and occasion. And United froze. By one of those strange quirks of fate that only football can throw up, Keegan was pitted against Ossie Ardiles, the man who was sacked to make way for him in United's first game in the Premiership. Unfortunately a favour by Keegan had back-fired on him. For five days before the season started Keegan had agreed to take United to Anfield for a testimonial for Liverpool stalwart Ronnie Whelan. The game had only been going a couple of minutes when Neil Ruddock clattered into Peter Beardsley and the United striker suffered a broken cheekbone. Keegan, Beardsley and United were not best pleased. At the time there was talk of Beardsley suing Ruddock but in the end the United player decided against it.

With Beardsley out until the middle of September Keegan had to act quickly and he just bought Welshman Malcolm Allen from Millwall in a £300,000 deal in time to be involved against Spurs. But it was a Cockney boy Teddy Sheringham who spoiled Keegan and United's big day and brought a faint smile to the lips of Ardiles when he scored the only goal of the game after 36 minutes. Liam O'Brien came on as a substitute and in the dying seconds crashed his free-kick against the post to almost salvage something for United.

United's first away trip was to Coventry – and Mick Quinn who had crossed swords with Keegan just after he moved from St James's Park to Highfield Road. Quinn got his big chance from the penalty spot after 35 minutes when Pavel Srnicek was sent off for a professional foul on Roy Wegerle but with his old mate Tommy Wright taking up a stance between the sticks the burly striker blazed his effort high into the demolition work behind the goal. But if Quinn blew it, another former United striker, Mick Harford, didn't, for just when it looked as though United's ten men were going to hold on for a deserved first point in the Premiership, Harford came on as substitute after 73 minutes and five minutes from time grabbed the winner with a looping header.

United did not even have the pleasure of scoring their first Premiership goal themselves when Liam O'Brien's free-kick was deflected into the net by Peter Atherton. O'Brien protested to me afterwards but it was definitely an own goal.

However, there was no doubting just who was the first United player to get his name on the Premiership score-sheet – none other than Andy Cole. Not many people – me included – gave Newcastle much hope at Old Trafford as Manchester United paraded their stars in Ryan Giggs, Paul Ince, Roy Keane, Andrei Kanchelskis, Bryan Robson and Mark Hughes. Giggs it was who gave Alex Ferguson's side the lead when he lashed in a free-kick five minutes before the interval. Surely the floodgates would open after the break and Newcastle would be sunk without a trace?

But no. Suddenly the Reds' renowned central defensive pairing of Steve Bruce and Gary Pallister seemed aware of Cole's pace. In the summer Keegan had brought in the splendidly named Nicodemos – Nicky for short – Papavasilou for a mere £125,000 from Ofi in Crete and it was the Cypriot who sent Cole in for his 70th-minute equaliser.

So Newcastle picked up an unexpected point and Keegan knew they had arrived. At the end of the season I asked Keegan when he knew that Newcastle were going to be a force in the Premiership and he told me: 'On the second Saturday of the season at Old Trafford. We had lost our first two games and we were expected to lose to the champions. I simply told the players that I believed in them. All they had to do was to believe in themselves. They then went out and took a point from Manchester United they richly deserved and after that we had no problem with their confidence.'

United picked up their first Premiership victory in their next match when Malcolm Allen conjured up the only goal of the game against Everton at St James's Park. Then came Alan Shearer at St James's Park on the following Sunday. I had spoken to him in the summer and he said I could have no idea how much playing at St James's Park meant to him. He added that while he had been one of the ball boys the night Kevin Keegan was whisked away by helicopter on the night of his testimonial, the only time he had actually played on his home-town pitch was in a six-a-side match as a kid. He was only substitute after his knee injury but Kenny Dalglish sent him on at the right time as within seven minutes he had cancelled out Andy Cole's opener with Blackburn's equaliser.

United completely outplayed Ipswich in their next game yet could only draw 1–1. Keegan's frustration turned to anger when he was hit on the head after an Ipswich fan banged on the United dug-out. Keegan entered the press conference saying he did not want to discuss the incident – and proceeded to talk about it and its implications for the next 20 minutes. So typical of Keegan.

He showed that he had unearthed another cut-price gem when Alex Mathie, a £250,000 signing from Morton in the close season, came on as a late substitute in the 4–2 home win over Sheffield Wednesday, made a goal for Andy Cole and scored one himself. Once again Sky Television were there. Keegan went on to describe Mathie's goal as 'world class'.

So everything Keegan touched at this time seemed to turn to gold or goals. Beardsley made an earlier than expected comeback in the 2–2 draw at Swindon. But suddenly it was Cole-the-Goal who was making the whole country sit up and take notice. His first hat-trick for United came in the 4–1 Coca-Cola Cup victory over Notts County.

> 'Andy Cole, Andy Cole, he hits the ball and scores
> a goal, Andy, Andy Cole.'

This ditty was to spill down from the terraces for the next 16 months. Cole made it a great double when he helped himself to another hat-trick in the second leg against Notts County in front of his whole family who are based in Nottingham. The United fans were still savouring the 7–1 hammering of Notts County when Keegan announced the following day that he was to sign a new contract which would keep him at St James's Park until the summer of 1996.

These were happy days for Keegan and United. But there were dark clouds on the horizon. Les Ferdinand came to St James's Park in the middle of October and led Queen's Park Rangers to a 2–1 win as United's 11-match unbeaten run came to an end with Malcolm Allen missing a penalty kick in the last minute.

The following Sunday United were at Southampton where they had not won since 1971–72. There was already an atmosphere at The Dell with the Saints fans baying for the head of their Gateshead-born manager Ian Branfoot. But even all this was forgotten as Keegan substituted Lee Clark. The midfielder angrily kicked physio Derek Wright's bag and headed off down the touchline. Keegan chased after him and dragged him back into the dug-out. Even the recalled Le Tissier's two goals in a 2–1 home win did not get as many headlines as Keegan's very public bust-up with Clark.

Amazingly, worse was to follow. Four days later United were at one of their least favourite hunting grounds for their Coca-Cola Cup third-round tie with Wimbledon. Keegan left Clark out even though it was his 21st birthday. There was also no Cole as United crashed out 2–1. I had sensed something was wrong when I rang Keegan at United's Selsdon Park headquarters on the morning of the match and he flatly refused to discuss any of his team plans.

During the match Keegan and Terry Mac hardly moved from their places at either side of the United dug-out as word filtered through that Cole had a 'hamstring injury'. At the post-match press conference it was Keegan himself who volunteered the information that Cole had gone missing. He then invited the press to go out in London and find his centre forward. He could easily have said that Cole had the flu or something and no one would have been any the wiser. But this wasn't Keegan's style. However he did storm out of the press conference.

Plans for Keegan to fly back from nearby Gatwick on one of the supporters' planes were hastily changed and I watched him board the team bus. For the second time in four days Keegan gagged his players – a contradiction of his often proud boast to me: 'We've got no secrets here.' After flying back on one of the supporters' planes I was at my desk at seven o'clock the next morning with nobody to speak to.

But I then became the first person to speak to Cole after having the brainwave of speaking to my counterpart in Bristol and obtaining the phone number of Andy's girlfriend in London. I got off to a bad start calling her Sheila, leaving her to tell me: 'My name's Shirley.' Andy came to the phone insisting that he had not walked out on the club but that he had told Keegan he was homesick. He said that Keegan flew off the handle and Cole told him he did not want to play. There was obviously now a problem between Cole and Keegan. I wrote the following day that United faced their biggest crisis since Keegan had walked out on them 19 months earlier.

Something had to be done and for once Keegan took a back seat. It was Vice-Chairman Freddie Shepherd, Director Douglas Hall and Chief Executive Freddie Fletcher who met Cole and his agent Paul Stretford in Jesmond. Early the next morning I got a phone call from a trusted source who would only say, 'There's peace in our time.'

Cole was the first to arrive at United's training ground at Durham. Then Keegan breezed in looking as though he did not have a care in the world. Cole looked relaxed as he waited outside Keegan's office. In those days the United boss gave us such open access we were able to watch the drama unfold. It all ended in smiles and handshakes but when I asked Keegan if he would alter anything in the past week he said, 'My job is to manage the playing side of this football club and if I had a choice I would not do anything different from what I have done.' For me these were the words of a strong manager who was singleminded in his desire to bring success to Newcastle United.

Keegan reinstated Cole and Clark the next day. True to form Cole scored and Peter Beardsley got a hat-trick as Wimbledon, winners over United just four days earlier in the Coca-Cola Cup, were crushed 4–0. After the game Keegan announced that United were back in business and they were on course to become a real force in the game. There wasn't one dissenting voice.

United's next match, a 3–1 win at Oldham in front of the Sky cameras, was also significant, for they played with such style and panache that Sky anchorman Richard Keys dubbed them The Entertainers. It was a name which was destined to stick. And how Keegan loved it. It typified everything he was trying to do at St James's Park.

There was even better to come in United's next match. By now Sky could not get enough of United and their game with Liverpool was switched to the Sunday afternoon – a snowy November Sunday afternoon. But not a single United fan felt the cold or even noticed the snow, for unbelievably United were three up in the first half hour – all scored by Cole from left-wing crosses involving Scott Sellars. Keegan sat back into the dug-out contentedly as the United fans chanted to their Liverpool counterparts, 'What's it like to be outclassed?' Later there were to be allegations that Liverpool keeper Bruce Grobbelaar had accepted a bribe to fix the result but nothing would have stopped Cole and United that day.

Another team outclassed were Sheffield United who were on the wrong end of a 4–0 drubbing at St James's Park as Keegan nicely guided his side into fourth spot behind Manchester United, Blackburn and Aston Villa – their highest placing so far in the FA Carling Premiership.

There was more good news off the pitch as St James's Park was confirmed as a venue for the 1996 European Championships. Then in December Keegan uttered the words every United fan wanted to hear as Graham Taylor resigned as England manager: 'I'm not interested.'

Just before Christmas Manchester United came to town and once again the two teams played out a 1–1 draw. It meant that Alex Ferguson's side stayed 13 points clear of Newcastle and Keegan sensed there was some disappointment among the fans. He quite rightly pointed out that if Newcastle United were disappointed about only drawing with Manchester United then they must be getting somewhere. Chairman Sir John Hall agreed. His message to the supporters was that the club had really come of age.

However, United ended the year with a defeat, losing 1–0 at Chelsea after a poor performance at Stamford Bridge. As usual Keegan did not beat about the bush, saying United had got what they deserved – nothing.

But normal service was soon resumed. When United won 2–1 at Norwich on 4 January the tributes really flowed in. Keegan said it was the best performance since he had become manager. Peter Beardsley rated it as one of the finest team displays he had ever played in. Norwich winger Ruel Fox, later to join Newcastle, said that United had taught them a lesson on their own pitch.

Only one person got it wrong. Me. I had tipped Norwich to win. So next day a huge picture appeared of me eating the previous night's *Evening Chronicle* – in effect eating my words. How many times did Keegan make people do that?

Coventry and Mick Quinn were sent packing in the FA Cup but United stumbled at home to one of Keegan's playing clubs, Southampton. In fact it was quite a day with the Saints appointing Keegan's old pals Alan Ball and Lawrie McMenemy to run the club only the day before and the BBC switching their *Match of the Day* cameras to St James's Park at the last minute. Keegan's former club were to prove to be a thorn in his side and Southampton won 2–1 to become the only team to do the double over United in their first season in the Premiership. But this wasn't all. United keeper Mike Hooper was beaten by a superb Matthew Le Tissier free-kick to give Southampton the winning goal five minutes from time. Hooper wasn't the first and he won't be the last to be caught out by one of Le Tissier's specials.

However, some United fans were not happy at the keeper Keegan had brought to St James's Park from another of his former clubs, Liverpool, at the end of September. Nor could they have been happy at United's shock FA Cup exit at the hands of First Division Luton Town, especially as they had home advantage over David Pleat's side before going out 2–0 in the replay at Kenilworth Road.

Keegan had paid Norwich £2.25 million for Ruel Fox but the winger had to wait for his debut because he was not eligible in the FA Cup. However, when Fox's debut did come in the Premiership game against Wimbledon at Selhurst Park it was completely overshadowed. Keegan had stripped Barry Venison of the captaincy following the now infamous Bournemouth wine bar incident and given the armband to Peter Beardsley. Beardsley it was who scored two penalties but United were flattered by the final 4–2 losing margin as they conceded more than two goals for the first time in 14 months.

Keegan described it as the most disappointing defeat of his time as manager of Newcastle United. Significant to what was to happen nearly three years later, Keegan said that he had not lost his managerial marbles but he had lost matches. When the weight of expectancy on you to succeed is as heavy as it was on Newcastle United, there were some who found setbacks difficult to take. Then, Keegan threatened to quit United, saying that the abuse and hate mail directed at Mike Hooper had forced him to drop the keeper. It was one of the few times I ever heard Kevin Keegan have a go at the United fans.

But if Keegan was forced to drop his keeper he had no problems at the other end of the field where United in general and Andy Cole in particular just could not stop scoring goals. Cole got a hat-trick against Coventry, following this up with the winner at Sheffield Wednesday. Yet, amazingly, he could not score as United stuck seven past Swindon Town.

Keegan decided he wanted his defence strengthened and he again broke the club's record when he paid Queen's Park Rangers £2.7 million for their long, blond-haired centre-half Darren Peacock. He had been on the trail of Peacock for some time and he knew he was the man when he asked Andy Cole who were the three best central defenders he had faced – and Peacock was one of them. At the press conference to announce his signing, Peacock laughed when I told him he was one of the few central defenders to stop Cole from scoring in the current season. It brought the house down when I told him he had stopped Coley – but couldn't stop Lee Clark, not exactly a prolific marksman, from scoring in United's 2–1 win at Loftus Road in the middle of January.

Cole was at it yet again on Peacock's United debut in the 3-0 home win over Norwich City at the end of March. He became the first player to reach 30 goals in the top flight since Clive Allen seven years earlier. In the following game at Leeds, Cole struck after only three minutes to make it 50 goals in as many games for United – a truly magnificent record. He was almost waiting for me in the Elland Road corridors after the match to tell me that he thought the best was yet to come.

But even Cole could not score in the drab goalless draw with a defence-minded Glenn Hoddle's Chelsea at St James's Park on Easter Monday. Yet United fans had not exactly been starved of goals. This was their first goalless draw for 57 matches – testimony to the way they played under Kevin Keegan.

Keegan and United had probably their most emotional day of the season when they went to Anfield in the middle of April – the fifth anniversary of the Hillsborough disaster which resulted in the deaths of 96 Liverpool supporters. On top of this it was the second-last game at Anfield before The Kop – probably the most famous end in football – was to be pulled down to make way for an all-seater section.

United had former Liverpool players in Keegan, Terry McDermott, Peter Beardsley, Barry Venison and Mike Hooper making a sentimental return to Anfield. McDermott and Beardsley laid a wreath at the Bill Shankly gates but United did not forget they had a job to do – and they did it superbly.

They won 2–0 and Cole equalled the United record held jointly by Hughie Gallacher and George Robledo of scoring 39 times in a season. However, one remarkable record slipped by almost unnoticed. Keegan had done the double over Liverpool. He had also done the double over Everton. A superb Merseyside double double in one season, and Keegan did it without conceding a goal in the four matches.

Cole's big moment finally came on a Wednesday night at St James's Park at the end of April when he became the first United player to score 40 goals in a season in the 5–1 drubbing over Aston Villa. Four minutes before the interval Cole hammered the ball past Nigel Spink. The crowd went wild. Every United outfield player raced to congratulate Cole.

But no one was more delighted than the man in the United dug-out – Kevin Keegan. Cole went on to make it 41 at the expense of his old team Arsenal in the final game of the season. It was a fantastic achievement by Cole. But Keegan knew that everything had been right for Cole. Peter Beardsley and Lee Clark had an almost telepathic understanding with Cole, and Scott Sellars knocked in some great crosses from the left which invited Cole to score. Deep down Keegan probably knew that Cole would never have another season like that. But nothing was further from everyone's minds as Keegan led United out on a lap of honour.

Keegan was almost embarrassed to do so. He hated parading in front of the fans without a trophy. But those fans had plenty of reasons to be happy, for a couple of days before the final game of the season Keegan signed an amazing ten-year contract. He was also elevated from being a mere manager to United's Director of Football. At the press conference to announce it all Keegan unveiled Arthur Cox and revealed that the manager who brought him to St James's Park back in 1982 was returning to the club.

It wasn't really a surprise. I had spotted Cox in the directors' box at Anfield in the middle of May. Knowing the way Keegan felt about him – the feeling was mutual – I guessed he was coming back. Cox had just quit as manager of Derby County where he had been successful after leaving St James's Park in 1984 because he had been suffering from a prolapsed disc in his back.

Of all the people I have met in the game I have never met anyone who loves football as much as Arthur Cox and it was just a matter of time before he returned. Where better than at United alongside Keegan? Strangely Keegan never gave Cox a title until the last close season when he made him chief scout. Cox brought a lot with him – including his catchphrase, 'Wish you well.' Keegan and Terry Mac took it up and never wasted the opportunity to give it an airing especially when one or the other was on television. In the end it used to drive everyone bonkers.

On his new ten-year deal Keegan said that the job felt right and he wanted to see it through. He said he wanted the players to know that he too was totally committed to the club. But I suspect there weren't too many people that really believed Keegan would see out another ten years at St James's Park. But for me, finishing third to Manchester United and Blackburn Rovers in his first season in the Premiership, which is regarded by many as the toughest – and best – league in the world, was one of Keegan's greatest achievements as manager of Newcastle United. He did it to the background of Sir John Hall talking about consolidating in the Premiership. Consolidation is a word Keegan does not recognise. My own worry was Newcastle United had made too much progress too fast.

But while there were no trophies on the table, Keegan had given the vast army of United fans something else to look forward to. Europe.

# 7

## EUROPE AND ALL THAT

KEVIN KEEGAN SAID it was going to be The Great Adventure. And it was. But it was much more than that. Newcastle United supporters will never forget their return to Europe after an absence of 17 years.

They say that Kevin Keegan never put any silverware on to the St James's Park table but I could swear that the First Division Championship trophy was made of silver. There is certainly no argument that Keegan put the club back on the European map. And just as in 1968–69 when they got into Europe for the first time in the old Inter-Cities Fairs Cup because of the one-club-per-city rule United needed help from elsewhere. They got it because of the war in Yugoslavia when teams from that country were disqualified from all European competitions. In June 1994 United finally received confirmation that they were in the UEFA Cup in 1995–96. The $64,000-question was could Kevin Keegan emulate Joe Harvey and win the competition?

After winning the Fairs Cup in 1969 United crashed out to Anderlecht in the following season and in 1970–71 they lost on penalties to Pecsi Dozsa in Hungary. There was a seven-year break before United got back into Europe in the now renamed UEFA Cup but after seeing off Dublin outfit Bohemians they lost both legs to Bastia who were one of the French representatives.

Not long after the Bastia defeat United sacked their manager

Richard Dinnis. But United supporters had tremendous memories of Europe and there was an enormous feeling of anticipation before the draw was made in Geneva. As had become their custom, United sent a high-powered delegation of Vice-Chairman Freddie Shepherd, Director Douglas Hall and General Manager Russell Cushing to Switzerland to keep an eye on the club's interests in the draw for the first round. Cushing it was who always flashed the news back to Tyneside via his trusty assistant Tony Toward who was poised to move into action at St James's Park.

When the news came it was welcome. Antwerp. Or to give them their proper title, Royal Antwerp. A hop across to Belgium suited everybody nicely. Antwerp had been Belgian champions on four occasions, although you had to go back to 1957 to find the last time they had won their own title. They had had a smattering of European experiences including a trip to Wembley for the Cup Winners' Cup final in 1993 where they had been beaten by Italy's Parma. Not surprisingly when the draw was made all press attention surrounded United's Belgian international Philippe Albert, and Albert did not let them down, pointing out that Antwerp had been bitter rivals in his time with Anderlecht.

However, Keegan quite rightly insisted that Antwerp should be forgotten for the meantime and the United players did him proud. By the time United jetted out of Newcastle airport on the Monday lunchtime they were top of the Premiership with five straight wins. They had achieved this without their influential skipper Peter Beardsley who had suffered a fracture of his cheekbone in the win over Leicester City in the opening game of the season.

United trained at Durham before heading for Newcastle airport and there was talk then that Beardsley could return against Antwerp the following night. But it wasn't until the whole party arrived at Antwerp airport that Keegan confirmed that Beardsley would play.

The press always travelled on the same plane as the official United party and directors under Keegan. But once we got to our destination we headed off in different directions and three different hotels. Keegan wanted no distractions and the system worked well. The night before every game in Europe, United trained on the opposing team's pitch and afterwards Keegan always made sure he and his players were available to the media.

Certainly being in Europe with Keegan was brilliant for the press. Even in his last season when he had cut back his press conferences he was absolutely superb in Sweden, Hungary and France for the games with Halmstads, Ferencvaros and Metz. So we all got into a little routine on these European trips and with the players at the front and the directors in the middle, the press took their seats at the back of the plane almost without being told.

But even pressmen who had been around for years were caught out by United's magnificent performance on that unforgettable night in Antwerp when the club marked its return to Europe with an amazing 5–0 victory over a shell-shocked Belgian side.

Keegan always wanted United to play their first leg in Europe away from home so he knew exactly what was required in front of the Geordie fans at St James's Park. But as expected the Toon Army always turned out in force in Europe under Keegan, and their behaviour was a credit to Keegan, themselves and the club. The 4,000 fans who travelled to Belgium's historic city of Antwerp with its breathtaking cathedrals were in good heart before the game even though they found they were going to watch the match in a rather dilapidated Bosuil Stadium. Believe it or not, Keegan declared himself nervous as the referee blew his whistle to get the game under way in Antwerp.

The big question on the lips of every fan was just what would be Keegan's strategy and tactics. Well, they soon had their answer. Amazingly, United were a goal up in 50 seconds, two up in eight minutes and before half-time they were as good as into the hat for the second round with their 3–0 lead. Robert Lee, who already had five goals under his belt, hit as brilliant a hat-trick as you could imagine as United sent a message around the rest of Europe with an unbelievable 5–0 victory. Amazingly, Lee's three goals were all headers. No wonder Lee emerged after the game to chide his colleagues saying that while he was not brilliant in the air he was a lot better than the rest of the United players thought he was.

But if Lee was delighted, Keegan was ecstatic. If the defeat at Blackburn Rovers on Boxing Day 1996 was the lowest I have ever seen Keegan then that night in Antwerp was probably the most elated I have ever seen him. As usual he was not short of words. He said it was frightening what Newcastle United could achieve with performances like that. Terry McDermott, who had won three European Cups with Liverpool, said that it was as good a one-off performance as he'd ever seen in European football.

Everyone knew the rules in Europe. Normal sides used to pull back and put up the shutters if they got an early goal away from home. But United were not a normal side that night in Antwerp. They only had one problem on the whole trip and that was when the party arrived back at Newcastle airport in the early hours. An immigration officer spotted a minor discrepancy in Marc Hottiger's passport and held the Swiss international up. Keegan moved in quickly to sort it all out.

Now there was only one question, would the United fans bother to turn up for the second leg a fortnight later when the tie was already over? You could bet your bottom dollar they would with just under 30,000 piling into St James's Park even though the game was beamed out live by BBC television.

Obviously with five goals in the bag it was always going to be difficult for United. Keegan knew this and he urged the United players to treat Antwerp with the respect they deserved. After all the Belgians weren't a bad side at all. He urged his players to forget about the first leg and go in against Antwerp as if they were playing them for the first time. He warned them that the Belgians would capitalise on any complacency they showed.

But Keegan need not have worried. United could not have been more professional. They won the second leg at St James's Park 5–2 to go through on a 10–2 aggregate, a club record in Europe, beating the 6–2 against Ujpest Dozsa in the 1969 Fairs Cup final. Andy Cole chipped in with a three-goal salvo to become the first United player to hit a hat-trick in three major competitions. Malcolm Macdonald, old SuperMac himself, had scored hat-tricks in three different competitions, though one of them was the Mickey Mouse Anglo-Italian Cup, while Cole's had come in the League, the Coca-Cola Cup and now the UEFA

Cup. The victory had Keegan enthusing that it would send shudders around the whole of Europe. He said that the players wanted more of it and that he had been very proud of his players over the two legs.

When the draw was made for the second round United were paired with Atletico Bilbao, and the way the draw fell United would have to go to the Basque country in Northern Spain for the second leg, with Keegan wishing it had been the other way around.

Away from Europe United were still unbeaten in the League and Coca-Cola Cup when the Spaniards arrived at St James's Park for the first leg. The fact that they wore red and white stripes, the colours of United's arch enemies Sunderland, only added to the occasion.

United had the boost of an early goal from Ruel Fox and when Cole was brought down Peter Beardsley made it two from the penalty spot with 11 minutes of the first half remaining. But it was Cole's goal 11 minutes into the second half which really got the fans going. It was a beautiful move with the ball going from Darren Peacock to Peter Beardsley who flicked on for Lee Clark to feed Fox out on the right. When the deliberately placed cross reached the middle, Cole, who was not particularly strong in the air, had no trouble heading in a picture goal.

United were 3–0 up with just over half an hour to go. They were in complete control. Surely the tie was over. Certainly the United supporters thought so as they started the Mexican Wave and tried to turn the night into a carnival. But the Spaniards, to their credit, never gave up. Substitute Suances caught United flat-footed, flicking the ball on for the impressive Ciganda to lift over the top of Pavel Srnicek to reduce the arrears after 71 minutes. The Mexican Wave was soon curbed but this did not prevent that man Suances heading a second goal for Bilbao 11 minutes from time. It could have been worse as the Spaniards had another chance to score. United hung on to a 3–2 win, but there wasn't a person in the ground or at home watching on television who did not know the significance of those two away goals.

Nobody knew better than Keegan. He was honest enough to admit that United had been naïve. All the talk after the game was that United should have shut up shop at 3–0. Yet playing defensively was something which was alien to Keegan. And United had not done badly under Keegan, had they?

United knew that they faced a Spanish Inquisition in Bilbao and that they would have to come up with the right answers. The tie was superbly poised as a spectacle yet the BBC surprisingly opted out of going to Bilbao for live coverage of the second leg and instead took in Aston Villa's game with Trabzonspor.

Two days before United jetted out to Spain they had to go to Old Trafford to take on Manchester United in a top of the Premiership clash. They went without Andy Cole, who the day before decided to rest his problem shins for a month, and they lost 2–0 – their first defeat of the season.

The second leg was played in Bilbao on Tuesday, 1 November, and when we arrived in Northern Spain on the Monday afternoon the sun was shining. But it was cloudy and overcast the day of the match as the two sets of fans proceeded to put on the biggest party I have ever seen. Basques and Geordies lined the traffic-free streets together in an amazing show of camaraderie.

I have never experiencd anything like the atmosphere when we got to the San Mames Stadium. The support the Atletico supporters gave their team was unbelievable, especially from those who did not have seats as they jumped up and down on the ground.

Quite frankly, I couldn't see how United could fail to crack in this atmosphere. Keegan pointed out that if United kept a clean sheet then they were through and a gritty United held out until the 66th minute when a shot from Ciganda took a deflection off visiting man-of-the-match Steve Howey and clickety-click they were out.

To be fair, with no Cole United hardly threatened the Bilbao goal all night, although there seemed to be one penalty claim turned down by Italian referee Angelo Amendella. So it was amen and goodnight for United. They lost 1–0 but Keegan knew that the tie had really been lost in the first leg at St James's Park.

It was again after midnight when the United party arrived back on Tyneside, and to this day when I close my eyes I can see a tired Kevin Keegan resting against the wall beside the baggage carousel, holding an impromptu press conference. Obviously he was down but he was far from being out – and he was positive as usual. He said that The Great Adventure was history now but Newcastle United wanted more of it. He added that a new chapter was about to begin for the club, that United were going to be at the top for a very very long time and that Europe had given them not just a platform to achieve this but also to become an institution. Stirring words indeed and I bet the United fans had a lump in their throats when they read their *Evening Chronicle* the following night.

Keegan's one hope was that the UEFA exit would not give United a Premiership hangover, but 18 days after losing in Spain United were beaten by Wimbledon at Selhurst Park and they lost the top spot never to regain it again that season. In the end United finished sixth and did not qualify for Europe. There was to be no Great Adventure in 1995–96. When United did get back into Europe two years later, six players – Pavel Srnicek, Darren Peacock, Steve Howey, Robert Lee, Steve Watson and Peter Beardsley – were still all in the 11 against Swedish part-timers Halmstads from the starting line-up in Bilbao. But there were some new faces. Exciting faces. Players who on their day could be counted among the best in the world. Alan Shearer, Faustino Asprilla, Les Ferdinand and Gallic genius David Ginola.

Keegan took a lot of the credit in the 4–0 victory over Halmstads, leaving out left back Robbie Elliott from the team which had beaten Spurs at White Hart Lane four days earlier to play three central defenders and bring in Colombian striker Asprilla. However, it was Ferdinand who got the ball rolling with his first goal in Europe, followed by a beauty from Asprilla. Philippe Albert came on for Steve Howey at the start of the second half and immediately helped himself to a goal with Peter Beardsley scoring in the way only he can score. The disappointment was that Alan Shearer did not get his name on the scoresheet.

Keegan was suitably impressed, which is more than can be said about the second leg in Southern Sweden when United, after being a goal up through an absolute belter from Ferdinand, went down 2–1 to two late goals. We knew that Keegan was angry when he opened his press conference by saying that he had not brought any of his players with him because he did not think any of them were good enough. He summed up United's performance in one word – 'Pitiful'. Not surprisingly Halmstads manager Tom Prahl gave United the thumbs down for the rest of the competition. But at least United were again in the hat for the next round when they were pulled out with Hungarian champions Ferencvaros.

As top-dogs Ferencvaros had actually taken part in the Champions Cup but their early elimination from this gave them the right to go into the UEFA Cup. As soon as the draw was made news started to filter through about the violent and racist reputation of the Ferencvaros supporters. Yet when we got to Budapest we found it a beautiful and fascinating city. For the first time in living memory instead of lazing around on the day of the match the press went off on a guided tour. We also had a guide of a different type to move from our palatial hotel overlooking the River Danube to the Ulloi Stadium.

I have been attacked by Chelsea fans inside Stamford Bridge and spat on at countless grounds in England but this was the first time I have feared for my safety as our police escort took us into the stadium. The atmosphere was intimidating to say the least and we had a situation where the members of the press were frightened to use the toilet because it was on the floor below among all the Ferencvaros fans.

Yet there was plenty of goodwill from the Ferencvaros fans towards Keegan. Hungarian legend Ferenc Puskas publicly told Keegan that he was one of the greatest players in the world and that he could go on to become one of the greatest managers.

Even Keegan could not prevent United from going two goals down after only 16 minutes following some really sloppy defending. To their credit United fought back with two excellent goals from Les Ferdinand and Alan Shearer although the strikers got some terrible treatment from the Ferencvaros defence and absolutely no protection from Swedish referee Leif Sundell. A Peter Beardsley mistake led to the Hungarians scoring again in the second half to run out 3–2 winners. Yet the drama wasn't over when Shearer came from an onside position to slide in a late effort – only for the linesman to raise his flag. What looked like a perfectly good United equaliser was ruled out.

Both Keegan and Shearer were understandably furious. When

I spoke to Shearer after the game he was still angry not only at his late goal being disallowed but also at the treatment that had been dished out to him and Ferdinand by the Ferencvaros defenders. He gave me a wonderful quote which just about went around the world the next day after Russian defender Szergei Kuznyecov had asked him for his shirt: 'I asked him why he wanted my shirt at the end of the game when he had been inside it all night.'

On the final whistle the Ferencvaros supporters had celebrated as if they had already won the tie. But both Keegan and Shearer knew differently. Keegan rasped that the tie would not be over until the 90 minutes back on Tyneside. And as usual Keegan saw plenty he liked about his side, saying that in the 25-minute spell in the first half when Shearer and Ferdinand had scored their goals, United could have beaten any team in the world. It was half past three in the morning when the United entourage touched down at Newcastle on this occasion, and they knew that as far as Europe was concerned the ball was still very much in their court.

Four days later came the mega-clash with Manchester United at St James's Park and a 5–0 victory that shook soccer to its very core. It was to be United's best performance of the season under Keegan, but the second leg with Ferencvaros was not far behind it.

By the second leg Shearer was in the middle of his recuperation following an operation on his groin and the Hungarians were happy at that. However, Keegan still had two men of the moment, David Ginola and Tino Asprilla. Asprilla especially loved the European stage and under Keegan played far better in the UEFA Cup than he did in the Premiership.

The Colombian duly got the first two goals either side of half-time which effectively put United into the third round. But it was a stunning goal from Ginola that not only Tyneside but the whole of the country was talking about that night.

The Frenchman had scored a stunner against Manchester United in the previous Premiership match at St James's Park. Yet this one was even better. When the Hungarians only half cleared a corner kick, Ginola, lurking on the edge of the penalty area, brought the ball down and hit the most amazing volley which screamed into the net. Ginola joked afterwards that you don't score goals like that every day – but he usually did, in training.

It was another joyous night under Keegan at St James's Park. Beaten Ferencvaros boss Zoltan Varga told United that they could be the best team in the world. Unlike Tom Prahl, the vanquished Halmstads manager, Varga thought United would go on and win the competition.

United were now in the last 16 and wanted to avoid some of the big boys like Inter Milan and Monaco in the draw for the third round. Keegan himself said he would have liked to play his old club Hamburg in the final. The popular choice among the players, press and fans was a trip to the Spanish sunshine island of Tenerife. Instead United got Metz. A freezing Metz.

United were still flying high at the top of the Premiership by the time they set off for Northern France and Keegan was still looking for some silverware on four fronts. Shearer went with the squad and even though it was less than a month since his operation there had been some talk over the weekend about the possibility of him playing in the first leg in Metz, especially as Les Ferdinand had suffered a depressed fracture of his cheekbone the previous Saturday against West Ham United. But the first thing Keegan did when he arrived at Newcastle airport on the Monday morning was to kill off any talk of Shearer playing. So for the first time in the season Keegan had to go in without his lethal strike force of Shearer and Ferdinand, who at the time had 19 goals between them.

Keegan gave no clues away as United trained as usual the night before in Metz's Stade Saint-Symphorian Stadium. It was a terrible night with the snow bleaching down on top of the freezing conditions. The United players could not get off the pitch quickly enough when Keegan finally called a halt. But not Keegan. Wearing some natty headwear the United boss gave at least half a dozen interviews to the media – French and English – when he must have been dying to jump into a hot bath.

It wasn't much warmer the following night and there had been talk during the day that the game was in danger of being called off. It went ahead with the viewers back home watching the game live on BBC amazed at the sight of some United fans in their black and white short-sleeved shirts.

Tino Asprilla, playing up front on his own, was soon to warm up those United supporters. When he was brought down in the area by Metz keeper Lionel Letizi it meant two things. The first was obviously a penalty and Letizi's booking meant he would miss the second leg at St James's Park. Miss is something Peter Beardsley did not do as the United skipper gave his side the lead after half an hour. David Batty typified a battling United spirit when after clearly being punched by Metz's Brazilian midfielder Isaias he needed four stitches in a cut eye at the interval.

Metz put United under pressure in the second half and when Pavel Srnicek failed to cut out a cross, Amari Traore headed the equaliser. The game ended 1–1. It was noticeable that when the United players came off Keegan shook their hands – but he let Srnicek go by without any acknowledgement. But Keegan was happy at the 1–1 draw – the first time United had avoided defeat on their travels under him since the first tie in Antwerp. He told his players that they were a credit to United and that he would have settled for a 1–1 draw before leaving Tyneside.

The second leg at St James's Park should have been a formality, but by now United's nerves were beginning to fray a bit. When the French outfit arrived United had failed to win any of their previous five games, and the previous two – a Coca-Cola Cup exit at Middlesbrough and a home Premiership defeat by Arsenal – were disasters.

Not surprisingly United lacked confidence against Metz, and it must be said that with their star performer Robert Pires having a field day they should have wrapped it all up before United found their man of the hour.

Tino Asprilla already had three UEFA Cup goals to his name but the two he grabbed in the space of two minutes late on against Metz were invaluable. United were hanging on and Keegan was ready to substitute Asprilla, replace him with Steve Watson and try to do something he had never done in his managerial career – play for the goalless draw which would have been enough. However, David Ginola indicated he was struggling and it was the Frenchman who gave way to Watson after 68 minutes. Asprilla stayed on and scored in the 80th and 82nd minute. However, the Colombian striker became over-excited in his celebrations of his opening goal, removing his shirt and making it into a flag, and was booked. This booking to go with his previous yellow card meant that Asprilla was suspended for United's next game in Europe. Not only that – in the dying minutes Asprilla pulled a hamstring and was out for the next two months. But as he was carried off on a stretcher Asprilla was still able to acknowledge the fans' cheers. It had been a typical quiet day at the office for the Colombian. As honest as usual, Keegan admitted that he was on the point of substituting his match-winner.

Just over one month later Keegan had resigned. The second leg with Metz was to be his last game as United boss in Europe. It was appropriate that Asprilla had helped him maintain his 100 per cent home European record.

Monaco was next and a visit to Monte Carlo. Only Keegan would not be there. It's hard to believe that United thought they were taking a gamble when they appointed Keegan as their manager back in February 1992. The only pity is that Keegan was not in Monte Carlo. He would have been only too ready to try to break the bank.

# 8

## COLE GOES AND EXIT EUROPE: 1994–95

IT WAS ANOTHER hectic close season even by Newcastle United's standards.

United's place in the UEFA Cup and their reappearance in Europe after an absence of 17 years was confirmed. Unfortunately, it only came about through teams from the former Yugoslavia being disqualified because of the war raging in their country.

United themselves were rapidly becoming a cosmopolitan side as Keegan's team-building kept pace with the development of the ground. In the summer it was the turn of the old Gallowgate end to be turned into a magnificent all-seater section.

Keegan himself was also busy in the summer commentating on the World Cup in America for Independent Television. But he was also busy keeping an eye on the World Cup for Newcastle United. He had spotted a full-back playing for Switzerland that he liked the look of. So after the World Cup he paid Sion £600,000 for their much-capped right-back Marc Hottiger. Another class defender, Philippe Albert, had also caught Keegan's eye in the States, especially the way the Belgian defender surged forward and scored a World Cup goal against Holland.

Keegan had a tremendous knack as a manager in that it did not take him long to weigh up a player. He told me once he went to Scotland to watch one foreigner play in a European game but that as soon as the player ran out of the tunnel he decided he wasn't what he was looking for.

However, Keegan knew that Albert was right for United. Persuading his club Anderlecht was another matter. United had been invited to take part in a three-team tournament with Rangers and Italian giants Sampdoria early in August and it was while they were in Glasgow that Keegan and Terry Mac were informed that Albert was available. Within three days Keegan was meeting Albert at a hotel after he had flown into the Leeds-Bradford airport from Brussels. He didn't take much persuading.

Now they say wherever you go you are bound to find a Geordie. Well, Albert brought one with him to England in the shape of Peter Harrison. Harrison had been a well-known player in top non-league circles in his native Tyneside but he was a bigger name out in Belgium. He had actually played alongside Albert as the two stoppers for Charleroi in the Belgian League. Harrison was – and still is despite being manager of Blyth Spartans – a United fanatic. Not surprisingly, Harrison did a great job selling United to Albert. The Belgian was sold on the club even before he met Keegan.

Keegan tried to pull off a third overseas signing before a ball was kicked but he could not get a work permit for American keeper Brad Freidel. Keegan and Sir John Hall lashed PFA chief Gordon Taylor who had accused them of trying to import cheap labour in Freidel. Yet Keegan could probably have done with big Brad, for Pavel Srnicek who had been sent off in the first away game of the previous season did not even last that long this time round, picking up a red card in the first game of the campaign against Leicester City at Filbert Street. The likeable Czech who had earlier saved a Mark Draper penalty brought down Julian Joachim and off he went. So too did Peter Beardsley who for the second time in 12 months fractured his cheekbone eight minutes from time. Keegan had been typically upbeat before the game insisting that the Premiership title was up for grabs and that United were one of the teams capable of taking it.

The big consolation for Keegan at Leicester was that United had started off with a 3–1 win. The Geordie fans were still chuckling – or should that be clucking – as they made their way back up the motorway after Robbie Elliott performed his 'funky chicken' dance when scoring United's third goal and his first competitive goal for the club.

Coventry were the first visitors to St James's Park and a resounding 4–0 victory saw United sitting pretty at the top of the Premiership – a position they were to keep until the middle of November.

Things were already hotting up. Robert Lee was called up by England although he later pulled out through injury. And, perhaps more significantly, so too was Barry Venison against America for his first cap despite being on the wrong side of 30.

Keegan had pulled off a master-stroke with Venison, who must have wondered if there was even going to be a place in the United side for him. New boy Marc Hottiger was in Venison's usual right-back role while there was no room at the centre of the defence where Steve Howey, Philippe Albert and Darren Peacock were all vying for places. But with Paul Bracewell not starting a game until Boxing Day because of his groin injury, Keegan gave Venison the defensive midfield role and he played it to perfection.

United showed just how far they too had come when bogey team Southampton had to make the long trek home on the wrong end of a 5–1 drubbing. When they won at Arsenal, United had been victorious in their opening six games in the top flight for the first time in their history. By the time Liverpool arrived at St James's Park United had won eight out of eight, including an astonishing 5–0 win over Antwerp in their return to Europe. Liverpool halted the hundred per cent record when Pavel Srnicek fumbled Ian Rush's 30-yard effort in a 1–1 home draw.

Keegan added Paul Kitson to his squad for £2.25 million but not before he showed Derby County that he was not prepared to be drawn into an auction for the striker.

October arrived with controversy exploding over the omission of Andy Cole from the England squad to play Romania. The whole question was whether Cole was fit or not. Later on Keegan admitted that he told Terry Venables that Cole was not 100 per cent fit because he was being bothered by his shins. Later events were to prove Keegan right again. A 1–0 victory over Crystal

Palace at Selhurst Park – it's Wimbledon that United can never beat on the South London ground – with Peter Beardsley scoring a wonder last-minute winner saw United five points clear at the top of the Premiership. There was another honour for Keegan when he was put in charge of the England under-21 side in the absence of Dave Sexton.

Keegan then picked up his first win over Manchester United in a 2–0 home Coca-Cola Cup success – and in doing so became the first United manager ever to win a cup-tie against Manchester United. Not only that but Newcastle set a club record of 18 consecutive unbeaten games starting with the 2–0 win over Arsenal in the final game of the previous season.

The fact that Alex Ferguson fielded a team full of kids did not worry the Newcastle fans a bit. But what was worrying Andy Cole was the problems he was having with his shins – the same problems that caused Keegan to keep him out of the England squad against Romania. Cole had only lasted 63 minutes in the Coca-Cola Cup-tie before giving way to Steve Guppy. Not only that but four days later unbeaten Newcastle were due at Old Trafford to take on Manchester United in a Premiership game.

Keegan, Cole and United physiotherapist Derek Wright had a difficult decision to make. By the Friday morning they had made it and Keegan said he would announce it at the lunchtime press conference, which was no good at all to my early *Evening Chronicle* editions. My face must have told him this for he suddenly blurted out that Cole was going to be rested for a month in a bid to solve the problem.

So Cole was missing when United went into the lions' den at Old Trafford and what was also missing when they came out was their unbeaten record. Alex Ferguson's side ran out 2–0 winners with the second home goal coming 14 minutes from time from a slip of an Irish lad who had only been on ten minutes as a substitute for Ryan Giggs – Keith Gillespie. It was weird considering what was going to take place just over ten weeks later that Gillespie should first come to the attention of Newcastle supporters on the day Cole's absence was put forward as one of the reasons for the first defeat of the season.

To make matters worse four days after the Manchester United set-back Newcastle went to Spain and were tumbled out of the

UEFA Cup by Atletico Bilbao, and that after being 3–0 ahead at one stage in the first leg at St James's Park.

The next three Premiership games without Cole brought three points against Queen's Park Rangers, a Monday night goalless draw in front of the Sky cameras at Nottingham Forest and the usual defeat by Wimbledon at Selhurst Park. Every game at Selhurst Park involving Wimbledon and United is full of talking points – and this one was no different. Vinnie Jones was sent off for two bookable offences. All five goals came in the first 36 minutes and Mick Harford was again to score the winner against United.

But, once again, Keegan turned out to be the talking point. To be fair to the man he had agreed to give a talk for charity deep down in the West Country and with about eight minutes to go including injury time he was clearly seen to leave his seat in the United dug-out, walk along the touchline and disappear down the tunnel. The official reason was later given that he had got a flyer to beat the traffic on his way west. But I wasn't so sure.

Keegan hated any of the United team saying anything before a game which might fire up the opposition. Well, Barry Venison had said a couple of things in the papers which we thought on the way down might find their way on to the Wimbledon dressing-room wall. So when Venison gave away a penalty late on, I was convinced that's why Keegan had walked out. In any case I wrote a comment piece in Monday's *Evening Chronicle* saying that I thought Keegan was wrong for leaving early. On the Saturday one of our elder statesmen in the press asked me if there had been any reaction to my criticism. I said there had not and in any case why should there be? Keegan never said a word to me about what I thought was constructive criticism.

The defeat in South London had not only knocked United off the top of the Premiership but saw them in third place behind Manchester United and Blackburn and by the time bottom-of-the-table Ipswich came to St James's Park on 26 November Keegan found it necessary to put out a we-have-slipped-but-we-are-hardly-on-the-slide message.

There had been good news in midweek when Steve Howey joined Peter Beardsley and Robert Lee in the England team to get his first cap in the game against Nigeria at Wembley – the first time United had ever had three players in the England side. And Cole was back against Ipswich after a five-match absence with United winning only one of those five games. Not surprisingly Cole bounced back with a goal. He left it late with just four minutes remaining. Ipswich, however, left it much later, Claus Thomsen equalising with just seconds to go.

Keegan took his frustrations out on Ipswich and their coach John Lyall, one of the most respected men in the game, for their defensive tactics. But what would have worried him more was the fact that Andy Cole had scored his last goal for Newcastle United, although obviously at the time nobody would have guessed this. But Keegan was delighted that, with no fewer than ten of his first team squad injured, United battled all the way for a 1–1 draw with Manchester City in the fourth round of the Coca-Cola Cup at Maine Road.

At the beginning of December came confirmation that United were now a club with world standing, for *World Soccer* magazine, after a poll of its readers, declared that United were the tenth best team in the world – and Keegan was the fifth best manager. But this was not enough for United to prevent Manchester City from gaining a shock 2–0 win in their Coca-Cola Cup fourth-round replay at St James's Park. The game was Cole's fifth without a goal.

When Manchester City came back to St James's Park to bring in another New Year, a lacklustre goalless draw meant that United had won only two of their last 14 games. They were out of the Coca-Cola Cup, out of Europe and had slipped down the table to fourth in the Premiership.

Keegan's answer was to try and buy a striker to play alongside Cole, who after the 1–1 FA Cup third-round draw with Blackburn Rovers at St James's Park, had gone nine league and Cup games without a goal. Queen's Park Rangers said no to a big bid for Les Ferdinand while Crystal Palace turned down a £4 million offer for Chris Armstrong. In any case the Newcastle-born striker said that he did not want to join United.

Then came the news which shook not only Tyneside but the whole of football. United had sold Andy Cole to Manchester United in exchange for £6 million and Keith Gillespie. Keegan believed that selling Cole was part of an overall plan to turn

United into an even better side, and once the shock and the initial anger subsided the vast majority of supporters backed their manager. Keegan told them it was his neck which was on the block and to judge him when he bought Cole's replacement. Les Ferdinand, Matthew Le Tissier, Dennis Bergkamp were just some of the names put forward as Cole's replacement. But not by Keegan. He never gave one hint.

Keegan still had his other United players to think of and amazingly Newcastle's next game was against . . . yes, Manchester United at St James's Park. Both Keegan and Alex Ferguson agreed at the time of the transfer that neither Cole nor Gillespie should be involved in what was sure to be an emotional match. Keegan knew that the Newcastle fans would be taunted over Cole by their Manchester United counterparts but a Paul Kitson equaliser meant that the two teams played out a 1–1 draw.

At this stage Newcastle's best chance of a trophy seemed to be in the FA Cup, even though they faced a difficult replay at Blackburn Rovers who at this stage were five points ahead of Manchester United in the Premiership. The odds were against United but not as high as they were for Marc Hottiger to score the first goal. But that's what the Swiss international did at 66–1. For once Alan Shearer did not score but another Geordie-boy did. Lee Clark was only starting his seventh game of the season because of a foot injury and with his old mate Andy Cole watching high in the Ewood Park stands the little midfielder rifled in the winner.

Keith Gillespie finally made his United debut when he came on at half-time in the goalless draw at Sheffield Wednesday and he got my man-of-the-match award on his win over Wimbledon four days later.

Then Paul Kitson, who had taken on Cole's striking role despite wearing the No 28 shirt, hit a brilliant hat-trick in the FA Cup fourth-round victory over Swansea at St James's Park. Cole himself could not have done better. But Kitson, who thought he had been badly done by in the press when he signed, refused to meet the media. Instead he slipped out of a back door still clutching the prized match ball.

Everton pressed the self-destruct button in the next game at St

James's Park when they had both Earl Barrett and Barry Horne sent off. United won 2–0.

United themselves were under strength when they went to London four days later to face Queen's Park Rangers and Les Ferdinand. Ferdie simply blew United away and scored twice in the first seven minutes in an easy 3–0 home win. Even at 3–0 down the United fans were magnificent and for a 20-minute spell they chanted non-stop to such an extent that my copytaker back in Newcastle, Sandy Patterson, was unable to hear me because of the noise.

United then picked themselves up off the floor to go on and beat Manchester City in the fifth round of the FA Cup at St James's Park. And who else should score two of the goals to go with a fluke from John Beresford in the 3–1 home win but Keith Gillespie? Three days earlier Gilly had passed his driving test and the day before celebrating his 20th birthday Keegan would have granted him the Freedom of Newcastle.

But there was another shock in store for Keegan and United fans when, at the end of February, everyone's favourite son Lee Clark said he would not be signing a new contract when his current deal expired in the summer. Clark had no axe to grind with Keegan. He simply wanted regular first-team football and he wasn't getting it at Newcastle. When Keegan told me of the situation he was obviously upset. So too was Clark. Keegan gave us permission to talk to him, and Clark pulled a crumpled hand-written statement out of his pocket. Before he read it to us he had gone off and sought out Arthur Cox to make sure it was all right.

Ipswich were beaten 2–0 in United's next match but they were so bad Charles Harrison, Metro Radio sports editor, put a bet on them at massive odds to lose 8–0 in their following game at Manchester United. They lost 9–0.

United themselves missed a great opportunity to boost their goals tally at Portman Road but seeing that this was their first win on their travels in the Premiership since the middle of October, Keegan was happy enough. There was another emotional night when Peter Beardsley failed a fitness test and Keegan recalled Lee Clark in the home game against West Ham early in March, and when Clark gave United their 17th-minute lead in a 2–0 success the fans went wild.

Courtesy of Newcastle Evening Chronicle

*Keegan on the night United won promotion at Grimsby with* (left to right)
*Brian Kilcline, Derek Fazackerley and Chris Guthrie*

Courtesy of Newcastle Evening Chronicle

*Keegan with Ossie Ardiles in the background in his first Premiership game*

Courtesy of Newcastle Evening Chronicle

*Keegan acknowledges the crowd at the end of the 1993–94 season*

Courtesy of Newcastle Evening Chronicle

*Confronting the United fans on the day he sold Andy Cole*

Courtesy of Newcastle Evening Chronicle

*Kevin with new signing Les Ferdinand*

Courtesy of Newcastle Evening Chronicle

*Friendly Foes: Keegan with Kenny Dalglish*

Courtesy of Newcastle Evening Chronicle

*A dejected Keegan after United had been pipped for the Championship by Manchester United*

Courtesy of Newcastle Evening Chronicle

*Last Gasp: United failed to beat Spurs in their final game of the 1995–96 season*

Courtesy of *Newcastle Evening Chronicle*

*Keegan with Newcastle chairman Sir John Hall*

Courtesy of *Newcastle Evening Chronicle*

*Oh No! Keegan looks as though he just cannot believe what is happening*

Courtesy of Newcastle Evening Chronicle

*At the press conference to announce Alan Shearer's signing for Newcastle*

Courtesy of Newcastle Evening Chronicle

*Keegan at Swan Hunter's shipyard on the Tyne*

*Courtesy of Newcastle Evening Chronicle*

*The end of the dream . . . . Keegan quits and the newspapers are soon sold out*

United next had to visit Everton in the sixth round of the FA Cup for a place in the semi-finals. It was a televised match on the Sunday and I arrived at United's training ground the day before just in time to see Peter Beardsley being led off by Derek Wright. United and Beardsley made optimistic noises but it was no surprise the following day when the skipper's name was missing off the team sheet. Also missing was grass on Goodison Park. In fact the pitch was terrible and it wasn't made any better when Everton keeper Neville Southall and some of the club's apprentices ploughed it up further before the game.

My old pal Joe Royle obviously knew what he was doing. Joe knew that there was no way Everton could match United for football. But what Everton had was Duncan Ferguson who could get way higher than any defender in the Premiership and the United back four were subject to an aerial bombardment throughout the match. Not surprisingly the only goal came in the 65th minute when Ferguson flicked on a David Unsworth free-kick. When it bounced off Marc Hottiger, Everton skipper Dave Watson headed it in. So another dream was over for Keegan and United. A disappointed Keegan did not linger long in the press conference.

United were still third in the Premiership and while they were too far behind Blackburn (12 points) and Manchester United (nine points) it was important they kept going to make sure they qualified for the UEFA Cup again. But after beating Arsenal, United and Keegan had yet another bad night on the south coast at Southampton. They were leading 1–0 with four minutes to go – yet lost 3–1. I flew back to Newcastle after the game and did not hang around waiting to hear what Keegan thought of that little lot. Later I discovered he had branded United a 'disgrace'.

The following day was transfer deadline day. There wasn't much activity at St James's Park. Late in the afternoon it was gleaned from Terry McDermott that Jason Drysdale had been sold to Swindon for £340,000. It wasn't until the following day that news emerged that United had signed Jimmy Crawford from Southern Ireland for £75,000. Then the *Evening Chronicle* learned that Keegan had made a dramatic bid to sign Les Ferdinand before the deadline. Earlier in April a national newspaper carried a report that United had switched £8.3

million from their bank into Blackburn's account in payment for Alan Shearer but Keegan dismissed this as the most ridiculous thing he had ever heard.

United had to go back to Everton again for a Premiership match on Good Friday and Keegan had to watch a gutless performance as Royle's men ran out 2–0 winners. Keegan kept his players in the dressing-room afterwards but told me he did not want to make public what he had said to them. He warned that he wanted to see some answers when Leeds United played at St James's Park on Easter Monday. As it happens United's 15-month unbeaten home Premiership record went for a Burton as Leeds won 2–1 and Keegan saw his men slip down the table to fifth.

Things were bad at this stage but if Keegan was down he never showed it. He was always liable to come up with a rib-tickling comment as he did when Radio Newcastle Sports Editor Andrew Dolby asked him what he knew about Gothenburg's Swedish international Jesper Blomqvist with whom United had been linked. Without stopping for breath he quipped: 'It's contagious and you can get tablets for it.' And then he was gone.

There was now the very real danger that United would not qualify again for Europe. Certainly since the departure of Cole, United had looked short of fire power and when they went to Maine Road for their penultimate away game of the season, they found themselves up against their goalkeeping coach, the 43-year-old John Burridge, for the whole of the second half. Yet Budgie hardly got his gloves dirty in an uninspiring goalless draw.

United's last away game was at Blackburn – and they proceeded to play Rovers off the park. Kenny Dalglish was indebted to his keeper Tim Flowers for keeping Blackburn in the game and predictably Alan Shearer notched a 29th-minute winner.

Shearer had done it to Keegan again. His goal virtually gave Blackburn the Premiership Championship. All United could do was to beat Crystal Palace in the final game and then watch Leeds United pip them for fifth place and take one of the UEFA Cup slots.

However, if Manchester United won the FA Cup final against

Everton at least Newcastle were in Europe again. But it was Everton who won the Cup leaving Manchester United to take the final place in the following season's UEFA Cup. Newcastle were out in the cold. To make matters worse for United their final sixth placing was the lowest they had been through the whole season. A season which had started with such promise ended in disappointment.

# 9

# SO CLOSE YET SO FAR AWAY: 1995–96

NEWCASTLE UNITED had finished sixth in the FA Carling Premiership and failed to qualify for Europe. Drastic measures were called for. That's why when Kevin Keegan jetted off across the Atlantic on holiday he gave his blessing to a most audacious bid – the attempted signing of Italian megastar Roberto Baggio in June 1995. And they were prepared to pay Juventus a staggering £9 million to bring the pony-tailed Buddhist to St James's Park. He was probably the best player in the world at the time.

It was such an audacious move that no one believed it. As usual the *Evening Chronicle* led the way with a series of exclusive stories on the Thursday and Friday. Most of the other newspapers ignored it all. It wasn't until the Saturday when Sir John Hall revealed that United had in fact been in Turin and had actually failed to get Baggio that the other papers realised they had been left with egg on their faces.

Even with Keegan away the United Chairman was happy to let the usual high-powered delegation of Vice-Chairman Freddie Shepherd, his director son Douglas and Chief Executive Freddie Fletcher go across to Italy. On this occasion they took Terry McDermott, who no doubt kept Keegan informed, and a local Italian restaurant owner as their interpreter.

It was Douglas Hall who had started it all earlier that month at the time Les Ferdinand signed for United. Douglas, ever the joker, left a United shirt with Baggio's name on it on the back seat of his car knowing it would be spotted by the television cameras and newspaper photographers. It was. But it was no wind-up. Freddie Shepherd sent a fax to Juventus asking them if Baggio was available and was told that he was not. However, undeterred, the United delegation headed off to Italy only to find that when they got to Turin nobody from Juventus would even meet them.

In the end a meeting was arranged with the top agent in Italy who, at first, did not keep the appointment. So the United party flew home apart from Douglas Hall who was linking up with his family for a holiday in Marbella. Douglas was told that Juventus wanted £8.5 million pounds which was in United's price range, but Baggio's demands for £64,000 a week were not and the deal never got off the ground.

Yet the summer had got off to a good start for Keegan and the United supporters. At the beginning of June, Keegan broke United's transfer record twice within the space of three days by signing defender Warren Barton for £4 million and then Les Ferdinand for £6 million. First it was Barton. It was an open secret, certainly to *Evening Chronicle* readers, that Keegan was more than keen on the Wimbledon defender. In the end United had to strike a deal with The Dons that they would sign him once the tax year ended, because of the London club's financial situation, and that's exactly what happened. At £4 million Barton became the most expensive defender in the game and there was talk that Ferdinand was following him through the door. However, when I asked Keegan about Ferdinand at the Barton press conference he chided me, saying it was Warren's day and he did not want to spoil it by talking about someone else. It was typical of Keegan and an example of his man management.

This was on the Tuesday and when Barton went off to link up with England for their Umbro Cup games Keegan finally unveiled Ferdinand on the Thursday. He paid Queen's Park Rangers £6 million for Ferdie and Keegan had finally got his replacement for Andy Cole. But it had taken Keegan and United 18 months to persuade Queen's Park Rangers supremo Richard

Thompson to let them have the powerful striker even though Thompson was a personal friend of the Halls. Yet even then United had to fight for Ferdinand after slapping in a £5.5 million offer for the England striker, as Brian Little at Aston Villa upped this to £6 million and that's what United had to pay. Ferdie himself made it clear that he wanted to join United instead of Aston Villa – and was subsequently booed whenever he played at Villa Park.

With Barton and Ferdinand in the bag Keegan was happy to go on holiday to Florida and let things take their course. But as soon as United failed to pull off the signing of Roberto Baggio the message came back to Tyneside from Orlando, 'Get Ginola.'

Now, I don't know how Keegan knew all about David Ginola. It could be that he remembered the French winger playing for Paris St Germain against Arsenal in the European Cup Winners' Cup. Or it could be that he studied him on one of the many videos the United boss always seemed to be carrying. But after pulling out of the deal for John Salako and with a question mark over the future of Scott Sellars, Keegan needed a left winger and that was the message which arrived at St James's Park.

Yet considering all the little snags Keegan had come across over the years in trying to bring in new talent for United it was surely ironical that the Ginola deal should go through without even the hint of a hitch while he was enjoying a holiday in Disneyworld. United agreed a £2.5 million fee for Ginola with Paris St Germain and the player and his beautiful wife Coraline soon presented themselves at the Gosforth Park Hotel. Arsenal and Celtic were also desperate for Ginola but the French star seemed determined to sign for United. He did. Indeed it only took United a couple of hours to agree a contract with Ginola – a mere blip compared with some negotiations.

So United had signed Ginola for £2.5 million. I must say that they had pulled off the greatest robbery of all time. I am on record as saying that Peter Beardsley is, in my view, the greatest player in Newcastle United's history. Yet in the first half of his first season, Ginola was the best player I have seen in a black and white shirt. Kevin Keegan had pulled off the steal of the century.

Just before the start of the season Keegan went into the lower divisions and paid Reading £1.575 million for their keeper Shaka Hislop. So another season started with United and their loyal fans again so full of optimism. The bookies again made United favourites for the FA Carling Premiership title.

Robert Lee, who has the knack of scoring important goals on big occasions, set another ball rolling with the first goal of the new season and Les Ferdinand marked his debut with a goal in the 3–0 home win over Coventry City. But it was Ginola – a debutant along with Ferdinand, Hislop and Barton – whose name was in the headlines the following morning. The Frenchman grabbed his first goal in England in the second away match at Sheffield Wednesday and it was a real belter with his right foot. Consequently United picked up a great opening double with Keegan being named the Premiership's Manager of the Month for August and Ginola the Player of the Month.

Les Ferdinand was ignored by Terry Venables for the friendly against Colombia but there was praise for the £6-Million Man from soccer legend Nat Lofthouse following a super headed goal at Bolton Wanderers, and after Ferdie had nodded in the winner at home to Middlesbrough, Ginola described him as the best header of a ball he had ever seen. Keegan's £6 million was already looking well spent. But even Ferdinand could not lay the Southampton bogey and he missed a sitter seven minutes from time as United suffered their usual fate at The Dell – the first game of the season they had not won.

However, Ginola was still the name on everybody's lips – apart from those of French team manager Aime Jacquet. Ginola was left out of the side to face Azerbaijan in the European Championships – a state of affairs which was to cloud his spell at United under Keegan. Manchester City right-back Richard Edghill became the first of many defenders that season to get sent off for a foul on Ginola, something which made the Frenchman unpopular on some grounds.

The name Tino Asprilla kept cropping up but Keegan's first foray into the transfer market was as a seller. Ruel Fox had asked for a transfer and when Spurs manager Gerry Francis offered Keegan the chance to make a massive profit on the winger he was on his way to White Hart Lane at the beginning of October for £4 million.

United had been top of the table right from the off and when Les Ferdinand inspired them to a 3–1 win over Everton at Goodison Park on 1 October they were four points clear of Aston Villa and Manchester United as well as making progress in the Coca-Cola Cup at the expense of Bristol City. Philippe Albert made his comeback in the second leg against City at St James's Park after being out since Christmas with a knee injury – and he scored while Ferdinand got the goal he wanted in a 3–2 win at his old club Queen's Park Rangers. The *Daily Mail* declared after the win in London, 'If only England played like Newcastle United' – a remarkable tribute to Keegan. And that was before United hammered Wimbledon 6–1 at St James's Park with Ferdie helping himself to his first hat-trick for the club.

But there was another storm in a teacup for Ginola after Stoke City manager Lou Macari accused the Frenchman of diving as his right-back Ian Clarkson was sent off for a second bookable offence in the 4–0 Coca-Cola Cup-tie victory at a rather hostile and intimidating Victoria Ground. It was to lead to a little slanging match between Keegan and Macari.

United were still going great guns but their critics warned they would come a cropper in November when they were due to play Liverpool twice, Blackburn Rovers and Leeds United and also go to Aston Villa. However, United saw off Liverpool and picked up three great points at St James's Park when Steve Watson scored a last minute winner. United had been second best and Keegan went straight across to his opposite number Roy Evans and 'apologised' for his team's victory.

After drawing at Aston Villa and beating Leeds United at home, United came up against Liverpool again, this time in a Coca-Cola Cup fourth-round tie at Anfield. Surely the best Keegan could have hoped for after Ferdinand was led off following a clash of heads was a draw? But Ferdie's 60th minute substitute, Steve Watson, scored the most incredible winner with 13 minutes remaining. Keegan called it a wonder goal and was so upbeat he said that United wanted to win everything they were in – the League, the Coca-Cola Cup and the FA Cup.

But United still could not win against Wimbledon in South London, although after the 3–3 draw Keegan quite rightly pointed out that it was the first away point he had gained against The Dons – and he still had a five-point advantage over Alex Ferguson at the top of the Premiership. And they had the chance to move 13 points clear when they went to Old Trafford to take on Manchester United two days after Christmas Day. But they froze on the night and Keegan was stunned into silence for one of the few times in his managerial career. To make matters worse for United and Keegan it was none other than Andy Cole who gave Manchester United the lead as early as five minutes before Roy Keane wrapped it up for Ferguson seven minutes into the second half. Keegan had seen United's lead cut back to seven points but he did not blast his side after what they all knew was a terrible show. Instead he kept his best words for the press conference saying, 'The circus came to town but we came without the lions and tigers.' It was the Manchester press who dashed off to their phones purring after a quote like that.

United welcomed in another New Year in style when David Ginola hit a gem after only 56 seconds as Arsenal were beaten 2–0 at St James's Park. However, United's season really began to go sour in the Coca-Cola Cup quarter-final tie with The Gunners at Highbury on 20 January. Before the match Keegan was installed as favourite for the England job after Terry Venables announced he was quitting after Euro 96. It finished with United out of the Coca-Cola Cup, Keegan and Terry McDermott in a fracas with Gunners boss Bruce Rioch and the sent-off David Ginola facing a three-match suspension – a suspension which was to keep the frustrated Frenchman kicking his heels for over a month. To be fair, on the night United did not perform and they did not deserve to win. But the manner of United's defeat left a nasty taste in the mouth of Keegan. Ginola and the Arsenal right back were old adversaries going back to the time the United winger was with Paris St Germain. Dixon knew exactly how much trouble Ginola can be.

Certainly Dixon gave Ginola the full treatment that night, completely cleaning out the Frenchman without even a free-kick being awarded on one occasion. Then Nigel Winterburn, Dixon's sparring partner, went through Ginola who was booked by referee Gerald Ashby for ungentlemanly conduct. The television playbacks showed that Winterburn, who had already been booked, had in fact committed a bad foul on Ginola and should have been sent off. Things did not improve in the second half and Ginola took out his own retribution by elbowing Dixon in the face. Even considering what had gone on before this was inexcusable by Ginola and off he had to go.

As he did the attention switched to the touchline where Keegan and Rioch had to be dragged apart. Rioch then started on Terry Mac as the police moved in. It was all very unsavoury in front of the glare of the live television cameras. But it was fascinating viewing – as long as you weren't a Newcastle United supporter. Arsenal went through with a goal a minute before half-time and a goal a minute from the end, both scored by Ian Wright.

After that red card at Highbury, Ginola, for me, was not the same exciting player for the rest of the season. That was bad enough but worse was to follow for United and Keegan. United had so very nearly gone out of the FA Cup at the first hurdle when they had been rescued by a last-minute goal from Les Ferdinand in their third-round tie with Chelsea at Stamford Bridge. After the game in London I sensed that Chelsea felt they were out, from manager Glenn Hoddle downwards. However, United still had to do it on the night in the replay.

In that replay United seemed harshly done by when Barnsley referee – there's something about Barnsley referees and United – Steve Lodge sent off Darren Peacock. The game went into extra time, then penalties. But when Peter Beardsley missed United's first spot kick Keegan must have guessed it was going to be curtains. It was.

So all United had to play for was the FA Carling Premiership – and they were nine points clear. Keegan now felt he needed some new blood to make sure, just as he had done with the First Division Championship three years earlier when he brought in Scott Sellars, Mark Robinson and Andy Cole. Just before Christmas Keegan let Sellars go to Bolton Wanderers for £750,000 and in the middle of January Marc Hottiger moved on to Everton for slightly less. Keegan next failed in a surprising bid to bring his former colleague Chris Waddle back to St James's Park from Sheffield Wednesday. Then suddenly two names were on everybody's lips: Tino Asprilla and David Batty. United slapped in a £7.5 million bid to Italian club Parma for Asprilla and made a £3 million take-it-or-leave-it offer to Blackburn Rovers for Batty.

United refused to make any comment about either deal and the speculation, as they say, was rife. With United keeping mum the tabloids had a field day with Asprilla. Guns, drugs, bar brawls, porn queens. And that was on a quiet day. Later I put it to Sir John Hall that perhaps it would have been best for United to come clean and keep the fans informed with a daily bulletin. But the United Chairman said that this had not been possible for several reasons, one of them being legal and also because the situation changed daily.

What did not change was Keegan. All the way through the Asprilla circus Keegan never wavered. He wanted the Colombian. End of story.

Later it transpired that Keegan wanted Asprilla and Swedish left winger Jesper Blomqvist. Keegan, Douglas Hall and Freddie Shepherd flew to Italy and then planned to move on to Sweden, although the latter part fell through. United agreed a £7.5 million fee for Asprilla.

While all this was going on Keegan learned that Alen Boksic was available at Lazio. At one stage the United party had to decide whether to sign both Asprilla and Boksic but in the end it was the Colombian who finally arrived at St James's Park after countless scares with the deal being off and on so many times it was hard to believe the saga was over.

The United supporters had every right to wonder if it had all been worth it. Yet Asprilla had a sensational introduction to English football when, despite only arriving in the country a couple of hours earlier, Keegan sent him on as a substitute at Middlesbrough. Within six minutes Asprilla had made the equaliser for a previously lacklustre United and unsettled the Boro to such an extent that Les Ferdinand was able to score a sloppy winner.

Asprilla and United did not do so well in the next game – a 2–0 defeat at West Ham – before they moved on to Manchester City for the last game in February. He duly got his first United goal in a thrilling 3–3 draw but he got involved in a couple of incidents with City's Keith Curle, first elbowing him in the face and then putting his head against his face. It didn't look good on television and Keegan stormed out of a post-match BBC interview with Tony Gubba and refused to go back on that channel again until just before he resigned. But as a journalist I know Gubba was only doing his job asking Keegan about the Asprilla incidents, and if he hadn't then his bosses would have wanted to know why.

The one good thing to come out of the trip to Manchester City was that in a corner of one of the public restaurants United finally tied up the signature of David Batty in a £3.75 million move from Blackburn Rovers. Batty was signed in time to play in the big one – the visit of Manchester United to St James's Park. It was the original six-pointer. A Newcastle victory would leave them seven points clear and within sight of the first Championship for 69 years. A Manchester United win would see Newcastle's lead cut to one point.

With the Sky Television air balloon drifting over the top of St James's Park it was a truly momentous occasion. Newcastle rose to it magnificently in the first half but were foiled time after time by Manchester United keeper Peter Schmeichel – the same Schmeichel Willie McFaul had tried to sign for Newcastle from Brondby nearly ten years before.

But it wasn't Schmeichel who got the headlines the next day. It was Alex Ferguson's *enfant terrible* Eric Cantona. There was a hushed silence as Philip Neville's cross drifted to the far post in the 51st minute where Cantona drove the ball down and into the net. This was the moment the Championship was won and lost in the eyes of a lot of people. Newcastle's lead of 12 points at the turn of the year was now down to a solitary point. How Keegan must have dreaded hearing those words '12 point lead'.

Alex Ferguson rang me from a garage near Warrington the next day on his way to Manchester airport for a trip to Italy to say that he had almost been overcome by the occasion and that Newcastle fans were not only a credit to their club but also to the game. He asked me to tell them he was not being patronising but the Newcastle supporters could not be consoled.

Newcastle bounced straight back with a 3–0 home Monday night win over West Ham but on the Saturday they were beaten 2–0 by Arsenal at Highbury and also lost their top of the table spot to Manchester United for the first time of the season. They were never to get it back. But there was still time for United to be involved in one of the greatest games ever seen in this country. Unfortunately for them they were the losers in a seven-goal thriller against Liverpool at Anfield. The tears flooded out unashamedly from the United fans at the shock of Stan Collymore's injury-time winner.

Six days later the television cameras panned in on the United fans again as one of their own, Blackburn's Geordie boy Graham Fenton, sunk them with two goals in the last five minutes. But this was nothing to Keegan's emotional outburst after United had beaten Leeds 1–0 in their penultimate away game of the season. Keegan had been annoyed at some of the comments made by Alex Ferguson about Leeds United and he sounded off on Sky after the game.

The first I knew about it was when one of Sky's anchormen came to me after the game and said: 'Alan, your man has just gone ballistic in there.' Sure enough Sky played it back time after time.

'The battle is still on. Manchester United haven't won this yet. Alex Ferguson has still got to go to Middlesbrough and get something.

'We are still fighting for this title and I'd love it, just love it, if we beat them.

'A lot of things have been said over the past few weeks – a lot of it slanderous. You have got to send Alex Ferguson a tape of this game. That's what he wanted, isn't it?'

On the final day of the season Manchester United would be champions if they won at Middlesbrough no matter what United did against Spurs at St James's Park. Incredibly, although it was denied at lunchtime of the Spurs game, Keegan offered his resignation to the directors of Newcastle United the night before. It was almost as though he knew that Manchester United would do it. They did of course. With Andy Cole scoring one of their goals.

All the good things United had achieved under Keegan that season were forgotten by the critics. The wonderful entertaining football, David Ginola, Les Ferdinand's 29 goals. Just one home league defeat. My theory that United had made too much progress too soon by finishing third in their first season in the Premiership seemed to be right. And after all, isn't finishing runners-up in the Premiership some feat? Keegan's critics highlighted the fact that United were going well before he signed Tino Asprilla and David Batty. To those critics I would only say one thing. Remember Southend.

# 10

## THE TRANSFER WHICH SHOCKED
## THE WORLD: ALAN SHEARER

KEVIN KEEGAN DID NOT buy anyone in the five months beforehand. He did not buy anyone in the five months afterwards. In between he bought Alan Shearer for £15 million, and surely there has never been a more talked about transfer or one which reverberated around the world in such a fashion. On the Richter scale it was ten and the only one which came anywhere near it was when Keegan sold Andy Cole to Manchester United 18 months earlier.

The story really began when Alan Shearer was born in Gosforth at the posh end of Newcastle on 13 August 1970. If ever someone was born to play for Newcastle United then that someone was Shearer. It's just that he went round the houses to do it and that it cost United a world record fee of £15 million for Kevin Keegan to bring him home.

It was appropriate too that it was Keegan who should bring Shearer home, much to the delight of every single Geordie no matter where he or she was, for as a 12-year-old Shearer had queued for five hours outside St James's Park to see Keegan make his debut for Newcastle United back in August 1982. Shearer was also one of those who sucked the ball into the famous Gallowgate End as Keegan had a winning debut scoring the only goal against Queen's Park Rangers.

Even Shearer himself could not emulate Keegan as United crashed 2–0 to Everton at Goodison Park on his league debut in a black and white shirt. Shearer had actually worn the black and white shirt when United gave him a trial shortly before he signed Associate Schoolboy Forms for Southampton in 1984. It *was* the black and white shirt he wore, not the green goalkeeper's jersey which has been so widely and wrongly reported. It makes a good yarn to say that Newcastle could have had Shearer for nothing had they not played him in goal. But it simply wasn't true. In a five-day trial with Newcastle Shearer only spent half an hour in goal.

As much as Shearer would have loved to have joined Newcastle at that time he chose a club at the other end of the country – Southampton. The reason was Jack Hixon, the scout who discovered him playing on Tyneside for Cramlington Juniors and who at the time was working for Southampton. Shearer and Hixon became great friends and there is hardly a day goes by that Shearer does not ring Hixon at his Whitley Bay home. Hixon watched with pride as Shearer gradually clawed his way to the top. The name of Shearer's game was goals.

In the summer of 1992 Shearer felt it was the time to move on to help his career progress. Keegan had just kept Newcastle in the old Second Division. He was looking for quality players, and they didn't come any better than Shearer. There is no doubt Keegan wanted Shearer and so too did the Newcastle United board.

I spoke to Shearer. He told me he would be prepared to talk to United. I ran a story to this extent, but Southampton's Geordie manager Ian Branfoot would not let the talks take place. He would not even let Keegan put in a bid. Branfoot claimed that no matter how much Keegan and Sir John Hall put on the table Kenny Dalglish and Jack Walker would top it at Blackburn. Branfoot told United that he had done a deal with Blackburn and there was nothing Keegan could do about it. Even Keegan was helpless. So Kenny Dalglish paid a world record fee of £3.6 million on 27 July 1992 to take Shearer to the then rather unfashionable Blackburn Rovers.

How Shearer made Keegan and United pay! On his first playing visit to his beloved St James's Park on 29 August 1993

Dalglish resisted the temptation to start with Shearer after he had just completed his recovery from his bad knee injury. But what a fairytale entry Shearer made to leave Keegan gasping in admiration. Shearer replaced Stuart Ripley after 68 minutes as United led by an Andy Cole goal. It was more like the entrance of a gladiator. Within seven minutes Shearer had stolen behind the United defence to glide the ball into the net and give Blackburn a 1–1 draw.

The following season he really drove United nuts. First he tucked in a penalty in a 1–1 draw at St James's Park. But it was in the return that Shearer really had Keegan tearing his hair out. United outplayed Blackburn only to see Shearer power in the only goal of the game with a header. It was a goal which all but meant it was Blackburn's Premiership Championship.

Right to the end Shearer continued to pile on the agony for Keegan whenever he found himself against his home-town team. In season 1995–96 United went to Ewood Park and came up against a rather lacklustre Blackburn on Monday, 8 April. It was just five days after the heartache of Anfield when United lost an absolutely pulsating match by the odd goal in seven to Liverpool. They desperately needed to win to put some heat on Manchester United and they looked as though they were going to get it when David Batty hit a blinder against his former club.

For once Shearer hadn't been at his best against United. Keegan must have been mightily relieved. Yet amazingly another Geordie-born player, Graham Fenton, came on after 71 minutes and scored two goals in the last five minutes to leave Keegan and United mortified. Like Shearer, Fenton had played for Cramlington Juniors. Shearer also had a hand in both Fenton's goals. It was almost unbelievable and there were tears spilled across the Ewood Park terraces by the masses of United fans. Most of them were in a state of shock. After he joined United Shearer admitted he was as sick as any of the Newcastle fans. But on the night he maintained a dignified silence. He was far too professional to get involved in anything like that.

There were hints at the end of that season that Shearer might be on the move. But Shearer shut everything out of his mind in the summer of Euro 96 apart from playing and scoring goals for England. I asked Les Ferdinand, who was with Shearer throughout Euro 96 and who was later to become his sparring partner at St James's Park, if Alan had mentioned any plans he had about his future and he insisted he had never said a single thing. Keegan and the United fans marvelled at Shearer in Euro 96. Little did they realise that every one of those five goals the Geordie boy scored as he helped England into the semi-finals would push up the price for them less than a month later.

With my connection with Newcastle United I had been able to get through to Shearer at his Formby home and spoke to him quite frequently in his days with Blackburn. I never forget what he said to me once. That one summer when he was back home in Gosforth and Sir John was in the process of rebuilding St James's Park he could stand it no more. So he jumped into his car and headed for the ground and simply drove round and round the stadium. I accepted then that it was just a matter of time before Alan Shearer wore the black and white of his home town.

This incident was never far from my thinking whenever Shearer's future was discussed. After Euro 96 Newcastle fans had to endure stories of Manchester United supporters sending faxes to the hotel Shearer was holidaying in with his wife and daughters on Paradise Island in the Bahamas. But Keegan was determined not to miss out on Shearer a second time. So were the Newcastle United board. Douglas Hall in particular seemed to think Shearer would be the signing which would really be the final piece in Newcastle United's jigsaw.

Douglas loved telling the story of how he was enjoying a meal with Freddie Shepherd in Michael Caine's famous West End restaurant, Langans, when who should come in but Shearer's manager at Blackburn – Kenny Dalglish. Anyone who knows Hall junior would know that this was too good an opportunity for Douglas to miss. So he wrote a huge figure on a table napkin and sent it across to Dalglish. Back came the reply – not enough. Douglas then sent a bottle of bubbly across to the laughing Dalglish. Little did they know what the future had in store for them.

But I always felt that there was one thing in store for Alan Shearer – Newcastle United – though this did not stop me from having a few laughs at Shearer's expense. I remember at the beginning of the 1995–96 season when it was clear that Keegan had signed another gem as David Ginola destroyed Stoke City in the Coca-Cola Cup at the Victoria Ground. The United directors sat directly in front of the glass-partitioned press box. I couldn't hear what Douglas was trying to say so he wrote out a message and held it up: 'Shearer's next.' I wrote back: 'He's not good enough.' I didn't want the Newcastle directors thinking they could impress me with any talk of big signings.

What never impresses me are the so-called exclusive transfers in our national papers, for newspapers have a reputation for getting transfer stories wrong. But the *Evening Chronicle* has a great track record on getting it right. But I did drop one clanger last summer. The journalist I respect more than any other, convinced me that Shearer was staying at Blackburn. I didn't know at the time but Blackburn owner Jack Walker had told him this. He carried the story in a national newspaper on Saturday, 20 July, as did another of the tabloids. I had advance notice and gave the story the treatment on the Saturday night. I had hardly arrived home that Saturday evening when the phone rang. It was Jack Hixon. A rather cagey Jack said that as far as he knew the story wasn't right. This could only have come from the man himself and I knew then that Alan Shearer would be joining Newcastle United, though this did not stop one woman from down the country writing to my editor and telling her it was time she sacked me.

United were off on their Far East tour on Friday, 26 July, and I was so sure he was coming I ran a couple of Shearer stories before then. Keegan hadn't been all that keen on the press accompanying United to Bangkok, Singapore and Osaka. I didn't tell him but I was half hoping I would not be going, for the Friday we flew out was actually the day of my son Mark's graduation at Sheffield University. It was a awful predicament for me but of course I had to go to the Far East.

Carl Liddle of the *South Shields Gazette* and I, the only two pressmen to start the trip, did not get the nod from United until two days before we left and while they went via Heathrow and Delhi, we travelled separately changing at Amsterdam. I had been to the Bahamas, Mexico and Barbados in the previous 12 months and I was bang up to date with my injections. Carl, bless him, wasn't so lucky. He was like a pin-cushion after all his injections and he could hardly sit down after a couple in one of the more tender parts of the body. He would never have forgiven Kevin Keegan had he stopped him going after he had gone through all that. So while I had a heavy heart, Carl had his problems in a different area as we jetted out of Newcastle airport.

We arrived in a wet and miserable Bangkok on the Saturday lunchtime. We were immediately ripped off by the taxi driver on the way from the airport to the magnificent five-star hotel we shared with United. What should have been a £5 fare suddenly became £40 and we had no option but to cough up as the taxi driver filled his tank in front of his cronies at a downtown Bangkok garage. When we got to our hotel and set about finding our bearings in the vast grounds we bumped into a couple of United players. They taunted us that while we were in Bangkok it was all going to happen back in England. The name Alan Shearer was mentioned but they knew nothing. They were only guessing.

We managed to find out that Kevin Keegan had been about to board the jumbo jet for Bangkok at Heathrow when his mobile rang. He did not get on the plane and instead disappeared out of Heathrow as the rest of the party, apart from a handful in the know, wondered just what was going on.

Obviously Keegan was up to something. Something big. I dared not think it was Shearer but we had a story that Keegan had gone off somewhere and it could only be a big transfer. It was only two o'clock in England. There was plenty of time to get it into the Pink on Saturday night. I rang back to Newcastle and spoke to John Stokoe who was acting Sports Editor of the Pink. We both agreed that it would be foolish to use what story we had. It would only alert the Sunday papers.

On the Saturday night and Sunday we never took our eyes off the United party in case Keegan turned up. On the Sunday teatime after an afternoon sleep I decided to go for a walk – and I nearly knocked Keegan over as he finally arrived in the hotel. Considering Keegan had not been keen on us going, tour organiser Paul Stretford was making frantic signals to me to keep out of the manager's way. I did. I hot-footed it out the back door and spent half an hour walking in a public park – much to the amusement of the locals.

On the Monday morning we went to watch United training on the ground next to the national stadium with the knowledge that at least we had a story up our sleeves about Keegan's mysterious movements. Unlike the rest of the United squad Keegan had hardly had the time to shake off his jet lag, having arrived in the Far East a matter of hours earlier. But he trained like a demon that morning in the searing and humid Bangkok heat.

While we were watching the training, directors Freddie Shepherd, Douglas Hall and Russell Jones came bounding into the training ground. They were in a great mood. But they usually were. As we sat and watched the training we even talked about Shearer. Or at least I did. At no time did they even hint or did I suspect anything. By noon – five o'clock in the morning back home – it was time to start thinking about returning to our hotel to phone over our stories.

By now Keegan was taking part in a full and gruelling nine-a-side out on the pitch. Amazingly at half-time he started signing autographs by the side of the track. We were ready to go when it was suggested we approach the manager just in case he had anything to tell us. Despite all the directors had done for the club only Keegan had the authority to give out any transfer news. Big or small.

As the senior man I was almost pushed out to meet Keegan. Not surprisingly the sweat was dripping off Kevin as he signed autographs the way he had always done in his life – with a flourish. I must admit my opening gambit was pathetic. It was a grovelling I-would-not-dream-of-interrupting-you-during-training-back-home-in-England opening shot but-I-know-you-missed-the-flight-for-some-reason.

At first Keegan said nothing. He continued signing autographs. Unknown to me the three directors and Terry McDermott had approached behind me. It was almost as though they were expecting some momentous announcement.

There was. When it came it hit me like a thunderbolt. 'We've signed Alan Shearer.' I was in a daze. I could see Keegan's lips moving but I could hardly believe what I was hearing. 'He's cost £15 million and he's signed a five-year contract. This is a signing for the people and fans of Newcastle so there will be no more statements until we get back home. And don't talk to or ask the players about Alan Shearer.'

Suddenly, Keegan was walking away. I don't think I was capable of asking him any questions but it didn't matter. Russell Jones said that now people would know why Newcastle wanted to build a stadium for 70,000 fans. Douglas Hall and Freddie Shepherd said nothing. They just grinned like Cheshire cats.

This was the biggest story of my life, yet I hadn't taken a note. I hadn't set my tape recorder. It had all happened so fast. It was not until I got back to the hotel that I recalled what Russell Jones had said. When we left the stadium I muttered to Paul Stretford that United had signed Shearer.

I looked at the players. They obviously didn't know. I found out later that Keegan had not told them about Shearer until they were on their bus and on the way back to the hotel.

It was still just after five in the morning back in England and we had a couple of anxious hours pacing the floor of our hotel. Would the story be in the Monday morning papers? Fortunately there wasn't even a mention of Shearer back home. It wasn't until seven o'clock – 2 p.m. in Bangkok – that I was able to tell *Evening Chronicle* News Editor David Bourn the news. He's as big a Newcastle fan as they come, yet considering the daze I had been in earlier I had a nerve telling him to calm down and stop acting like a fan as he celebrated the news.

When I finally got the story over I slumped on to the bed. But the phone rang straight away. It was Douglas Hall. He said he had been frantically trying to get me but my phone was constantly engaged. He said they had only been pulling my leg. They hadn't signed Shearer. I could not say anything. All sorts of horrors flashed through my mind. Including my P45. I knew Keegan and Terry McDermott were two of the biggest wind-up merchants in the business but in those split seconds I tried to assure myself that they were always serious about their football. Surely not? I was in a panic. Then suddenly I heard Douglas Hall and Freddie Shepherd laughing down the phone. I would gladly have killed them.

Once the news hit England the telephone never stopped ringing. We sat in our hotel room and watched it beamed over on

CNN. We knew it would be absolute chaos back in England, that the United fans would be going crazy.

The day after the announcement of the signing there was a knock on our hotel room door. Standing there was my old friend Neil Templeman, a Tyneside businessman who was one of United's breed of superfans. When he heard news of the signing Neil jumped straight on a plane and headed for Bangkok. That's what Keegan's signing of Shearer meant to him.

On the Wednesday morning after the big news we all switched to Singapore, and there to greet us were the members of the national press who had hastily been dispatched to the Far East. Included in their number was that journalist colleague of mine, a rather sheepish colleague – the one who had told me Shearer would be staying at Blackburn. He still insisted his story was right at the time because Jack Walker had told him so. Whether this was before or after Shearer flew secretly to see Jack Walker I don't know. It must have been the hardest thing he had ever done for Shearer to tell Walker he was leaving Blackburn.

Juventus, Manchester United and Newcastle were the three options open to Shearer once he decided to walk away from Ewood Park. He did not bother to talk to the Italians and knowing how much he wanted to come home I was surprised Shearer had hush-hush talks with Alex Ferguson. But once he talked to his boyhood hero Keegan it was all over bar the shouting. When you are a Geordie boy even European champions and England's double winners cannot compete with the pull of the Tyne. And Kevin Keegan.

With Keegan in their midst United were already big news in the Far East and once Shearer was added to their number it became a circus. It was pandemonium. Keegan put a gag on Shearer and on everyone else for that matter, and when I accidentally bumped into Shearer in the gym in Traders, our magnificent hotel in Singapore, I was manhandled away by a security guard. In fact when the national boys arrived in Singapore it was already too late. The big story had gone. As usual true to his word, Keegan refused to talk about the Shearer situation until we returned home.

I didn't care. Kevin Keegan had given me the biggest story so far in my career. Little did I know that while I would get other big stories from elsewhere, this would be the last big story Kevin Keegan would ever give me, or that I would get only one bigger. His resignation.

# 11

## THE BEGINNING OF THE END: 1996–97

WE WERE GOOD enough to finish runners-up without Alan Shearer. So with him we are surely good enough to win the Premiership. That was Newcastle United's John Beresford's view of the new season. Not surprisingly, with Shearer Newcastle United were probably the most talked about team in the world.

But there were already signs that things were perhaps not as they should be. I arrived back home from holiday in the summer of 1996 to be confronted by a rather concerned Paul New. The Sports Editor told me that United had appointed one of my former Metro Radio pals, Graham Courtney, as press officer. Instead of being available every day to the media, as he had previously been, Keegan was only going to speak to the press immediately before and immediately after a game. Not only this, but if you wanted to interview a player you had to go through Graham Courtney. All this was written in stone in an official memo sent to all the press by United and signed by Keegan and Chief Executive Freddie Fletcher. Quite naturally the press were not exactly overjoyed. But we had to live with it. We all knew it was pointless complaining. Once Kevin Keegan made his mind up about something, there was no changing it.

So the new system was implemented and it was still in operation when Keegan quit. To be fair, Keegan was still at his scintillating best at his press conferences early in the season. I could usually get enough from his post-match press conference on a Wednesday night to last the rest of the week. It wasn't until United went through that seven-match Premiership spell without a win just before Christmas that Keegan went into his shell.

I detected Keegan was not his usual bubbling self at the Alan Shearer signing press conference, or should that be circus? For me, Keegan did not seem as happy as he should have been as he paraded his world record buy. And when he made his little speech not many people picked up the fact that Keegan seemed to thank everyone but the men who mattered most. The club's directors.

Was it an oversight? Or for some reason had Keegan decided not to say a public thank you to the men who never said no to him? I don't suppose we will ever know. United had started their 1996–97 season with an 11-day tour of the Far East and I must say that it was a mistake. Don't get me wrong. The people in Thailand, Singapore and Japan were fantastic. It was a great public relations exercise, especially when Alan Shearer arrived in Singapore, and the players of Newcastle United were a credit to themselves and the club.

Despite the humidity, Keegan, Terry McDermott and Chris McMenemy really worked the players hard. United responded by beating Thailand 2–1 in Bangkok's national stadium and followed this up with a 5–0 hammering of the Singapore S League. And when they were beaten 3–1 by Gamba in Japan's second city Osaka, Keegan showed just how much he hated losing by giving his players a public blasting.

Quite frankly I thought he went over the top a bit, but by now nothing surprised me. Off the field the only real hiccup in the Far East came in Japan when Tino Asprilla was refused admission into the country at Osaka airport. The Colombian's reputation and that of his South American homeland had obviously preceded him. Keegan, who had had a bad experience as a player at Belgrade airport when England went to play Yugoslavia and he fell foul of the local militia, was in no mood for using his own immense reputation by arguing with the Japanese authorities. Instead, he whisked the rest of the squad away and left General

Manager Russell Cushing and Tour Manager Paul Stretford to sort things out.

When Asprilla finally arrived at the team hotel three hours later, he found Philippe Albert at the reception complaining that his feet were left sticking out of the bottom of the bed. The rooms were small in Japan, but Keegan was happy to let the players share as he felt it was good for them to have a little bit of discomfort. Later in the bar, I heard that Keegan had threatened to pull the plug on the tour over the Asprilla incident, but because I was eavesdropping I felt I should not report this and it never came out. Nor did the fact that some of the players felt that the trip to the Far East had taken too much out of them so close to the start of the season.

I had a bout of bronchitis earlier in the summer and as soon as I came home from the Far East it returned. I read somewhere that for every hour you are in the air, you need a day to recover from it. Well, when United arrived back at Newcastle airport there were just 12 days to the start of the Premiership season. Not only that, but United had two other trips to make, as well as the little matter of the Charity Shield with Manchester United at Wembley.

Either side of the Charity Shield on Sunday, 11 August, United played Lincoln City at Sincil Bank on the Friday night, and the following Tuesday – just four days before their Premiership opener at Everton – the whole entourage headed off to Belgium to play Anderlecht in Brussels. These were games United had arranged with Lincoln as part of the deal which brought Darren Huckerby to Tyneside, and with Anderlecht as part of the Philippe Albert transfer.

United could have done without them, but Keegan had given his word to Lincoln and Anderlecht. And Kevin Keegan never went back on his word. However, Les Ferdinand, as strong and fit a player as there was in the United squad, went down sick and missed the game at Lincoln City on the Friday night, and the way they played at Wembley, the whole United team looked as though they were ailing. Manchester United not only beat them 4-0, they humiliated them.

Yet the day had started in a great fashion. How the United fans loved it as they tumbled down Wembley Way. There wasn't a

Manchester United fan to be seen until they all suddenly appeared in the stadium before the kick-off. When the two teams appeared it was Terry McDermott who led United out. It was a typical Keegan gesture, despite Terry Mac's protests. But it was Keegan himself who faced the media after what can only be called a shambles in our national stadium. In another magnanimous gesture, Keegan pointed the finger at himself for picking the wrong team.

Keegan had kept his side locked in the Wembley dressing-room for almost an hour after the embarrassing defeat by Manchester United. He was hard on his players. He was hard on himself. He used a couple of words I had never heard him use before when discussing Newcastle United. He did not actually call the United players prima donnas, but what he did say was that he did not like prima donnas. He said he did not like them as a player and that he would not put up with them as a manager. However, Kegan added significantly that he had to be careful not to destroy everything after one performance. Yet Wembley most certainly brought Newcastle United down to earth – not just the players but the manager as well. Keegan's parting shot at Wembley was that Newcastle United might be stronger for the experience. The defeat at Wembley and the manner in which United capitulated hurt Keegan. He would love to have gone back to Wembley one day and erase the memory, but he never got the chance.

After winning in Brussels, surely all that was needed was a good result against Everton at Goodison Park? It wasn't to be as referee Mike Reed chalked off what appeared to be a good Shearer goal and United went down 2–0. Keegan's post-match press conference was over in a couple of minutes. He even went as far as to gag the players – something I can only recall him doing a couple of times before. Perhaps this was the first sign of things to come. In many people's eyes, to slap a press gag on your players after just one game smacked of panic.

United still looked as though they were suffering from the effects of the Far East tour, judging by the way they played in their first home game against Wimbledon. Alan Shearer duly got his first competitive goal for United in the closing stages, direct from a free-kick, to go with an early stunning effort from David

Batty. Yet just before Shearer's clincher a terrible blunder by the linesman, who wrongly flagged for offside, prevented Wimbledon from equalising at 1–1. There was not any doubt in anybody's mind that had the goal counted, then United would not have won.

Saturday saw the table-topping Sheffield Wednesday arrive at St James's Park. Now, as far as tactics are concerned, Keegan was never in the same class as David Pleat and both men knew it. But it was a late defensive error from Steve Watson which handed Pleat and Sheffield Wednesday victory.

In the previous season United had only lost one Premiership game at St James's Park, and this was to champions Manchester United. Yet here we were in 1996–97 with just two home games gone and United had already lost in front of their own fans. Keegan again hammered his men in the post-match press conference. He said the performance was as bad as any at home in all his time as manager. I didn't agree. There had been much worse than that in my opinion, but it perhaps showed the way Keegan was thinking. United's poor start to the season suddenly put a question mark over the future of Kevin Keegan at St James's Park in the eyes of the bookies. For William Hill slashed the odds on Keegan no longer being manager at the end of the season as early as the end of August.

United had to pick themselves up. And where did they have to go? Just down the road to derby rivals Sunderland, who had surprised everyone by making a good start to their Premiership season. All summer the 'David Ginola for Barcelona' stories had been simmering, and they weren't without foundation with involvement from the player's agent. I heard that Ginola was the player under threat of being dropped as Keegan mulled over his team for this vital derby match. I also heard from the players that until a couple of hours before the kick-off, Ginola was out and three central defenders, Philippe Albert, Darren Peacock and Steve Howey were in. Yet when the teams emerged, Ginola was in and Albert was out. It was an inspired piece of team selection from Keegan as Ginola provided the corner kick from which Les Ferdinand headed the winner.

Keegan had done what no United manager had done since 1913 in United's last derby at Roker Park, and that was to guide

Newcastle United to a win on Wearside after they had been behind. But this did not mean that Keegan was in a happy mood in the Roker press room. No one had criticised United more for their showing against Sheffield Wednesday yet his post-match press conference took the we-rammed-the-criticism-down-your-throats attitude. He chided the press that this wasn't the result they had wanted. The Sunderland press had a field day at this fit of pique from Keegan when he stormed out of the press conference.

Things were going again on the field. United strung a run of seven Premiership wins together. They were going well in Europe, beating Sweden's Halmstads, Ferencvaros of Hungary and Metz of France. Les Ferdinand and Alan Shearer suddenly started scoring goals in what was rapidly looking like a superb strike force. There had been doubters but Keegan wasn't among them. He was delighted when Shearer's goal at Derby County took United to the top of the table for the first time in season 1996–97 on 12 October.

Nobody, least of all Keegan himself, would have guessed that this was going to be the last time he would lead United to an away league victory, even though he was going to be manager for nearly another three months. After Derby, United's next league game was at St James's Park against Manchester United, the only team Keegan had not beaten in a Premiership match. But Keegan was to have his greatest day as manager, as Newcastle wiped out the nightmare of that Charity Cup defeat with a sensational 5–0 drubbing of the champions.

Newcastle fans woke up the next morning and wondered if they had dreamt it all. They hadn't. But Keegan's dreams of the Championship began to fade. At places like Nottingham Forest and Coventry. And as those Premiership matches without a win kept piling up, the demons must have started dancing away in Keegan's mind.

The euphoria at the way United had handed out that 5–0 drubbing to Manchester United subsided a trifle four days later when it was decided that Alan Shearer was to have an operation on his groin. Shearer was expected to be out for six to eight weeks and it was a huge blow to Keegan even though his £15 million man was back in action after exactly one month.

Shearer was back in time to play in the Coca-Cola Cup fourth-round tie against Middlesbrough at the Riverside Stadium at the end of November, but his goal was not enough to prevent United from slumping to a 3–1 defeat. It was Keegan's only derby defeat as a manager but no one connected with United wanted to talk to the newspapers afer the game. I can never fathom out why they always wanted to take it out on the press. In 17 years on the St James's Park beat I have yet to leap off the press benches and nod the ball into the back of the United net.

What the press had to do next was report that a ten-man Arsenal – their inspirational skipper Tony Adams was sent off after 20 minutes – had beaten United at St James's Park. United were no longer the bookies' favourites to win the Premiership title.

Keegan made changes to his backroom staff as he looked at every option to help improve United. United's defence had been maligned for some time although it was never as bad as some people tried to make out. It was a case of 'give a dog a bad name'. But in any case at the end of October Keegan brought in Mark Lawrenson, who in his days with Liverpool and the Republic of Ireland had been one of the finest defenders in the game. Yes, the same Lawrenson who caused Keegan to decide to retire back in January 1984.

Lawrenson, who had managed Oxford, had been working in the media, especially on Radio 5 and, like a lot of pressmen, had criticised Keegan when United had lost that 12-point lead to Manchester United. But it had been constructive criticism and Keegan was obviously prepared – if not to ignore it – to forget it as he welcomed Lawro into the fold. Lawrenson was joined not long after by Peter Bonetti, who moved in as goalkeeping coach after John Burridge moved out. Keegan had a big coaching staff and in some grounds there wasn't enough room for them in the dug-out.

Just before every Christmas Sir John Hall and his directors entertain the press at St James's Park. Keegan and Terry McDermott and some of his coaching staff normally used to attend. But on this occasion United were playing at Coventry the following day and by the time we were starting to tuck into our prawn cocktails, Keegan was already on the team bus on his way to the overnight base in the Midlands.

Sir John always gave a stunning speech which was followed by an equally stirring reply from one of the senior members of the press. I only half heard Sir John's speech because I nipped behind a partition to pick up some news of the Sky Blues from Adam Dent, my counterpart in Coventry. But I got the gist of it all. I must confess when I picked the morning papers up a couple of days later I was surprised to find that they had taken a Keegan-must-win-something-or-else ultimatum from his Chairman.

But I don't suppose I was as surprised as Sir John. In my view, he had been completely misrepresented in the reporting of his speech. Certainly when there was another meeting of the press a couple of days later for United to unveil plans of their new stadium, an angry Sir John was at pains to point this out. But the damage had probably been done. For while Sir John's remarks were innocuous in a general context, they must have been a hammer blow to Keegan in his distressed state.

As usual, there were highs and lows for Keegan and United. A high when Alan Shearer was named as England's captain. A low when Tino Asprilla scored the winner for Colombia against Ecuador, but then arrived back in England a couple of days late. A high when David Batty earned rave reviews and the man of the match for his display as England beat Georgia in Tbilisi in their World Cup qualifier. A low when it was realised that Steve Howey was going to miss almost the rest of the season with a calf problem. A low for Keegan when Lee Clark asked to be put on the transfer list because he wanted to play first-team football.

In the end, when the lows started to outnumber the highs, Keegan decided to end his love affair with Newcastle United. It was a marriage made in heaven and the honeymoon lasted the seven years Keegan spent on Tyneside, as first a player and captain and then as manager. But then Keegan got the seven-year itch and, as in all marriages, there was the odd tiff. Yet Keegan was always prepared to kiss and make up. Until the final split.

Kevin Keegan is the most positive man I have met in football. I knew there had been the odd problem and I knew that Keegan was as low as I had ever seen him. Yet I still felt he would ride the latest storm; not only this, but come bouncing back stronger than ever. I was wrong. It was over. In my view, while Sir John Hall runs him close, nobody in the history of Newcastle United has done more for the club than Keegan.

But life for Newcastle United without Keegan will go on. Indeed, exactly a week after Keegan quit, Kenny Dalglish was installed as his successor. Five years earlier Keegan was probably the only man in the world who could have rescued Newcastle United. Well, Dalglish was probably the only manager capable of replacing Keegan.

And Keegan? No one need worry about him. It is easy to say that he is a winner. But this is being disrespectful to a great man. Everything Kevin Keegan has achieved, he has achieved through hard work. That's why he will succeed in whatever he attempts in the future. I wish him well.

# 12

## KEEGAN THE MANAGER

KEVIN KEEGAN BOUNCED back into football like a breath of fresh air. You would have thought he had never been away as he swapped the golf course of Marbella for the hot seat at St James's Park.

That is after he picked his first team for the game with Bristol City, for when he announced it to the press it only had ten players. How he loved to recount this as he moved from rookie manager to one of the best bosses in the game.

He did it all his way. The Monday after that opening victory over Bristol City I went to see Keegan at the club's then training ground at Benwell. I told him that I was prepared to help him in any way I could. He never once asked for any help. Managers have their own ideas. Their own way of doing things. When Jim Smith was manager, Mark McGhee rang me from Scotland. He had been at St James's Park as a player earlier in his career and he was keen to come back. I was the intermediary between Smith and McGhee and the Scot came back for a second and more successful spell on Tyneside. But there was none of this with Keegan, and even the old habit of feeding the United manager with as much information on the opposition, including their likely team, went by the board. Kevin Keegan never worried too much about the opposition. He was always more concerned about his own team. Judging by the results he achieved, perhaps this was not a bad policy.

Another plus point for Keegan the manager was his policy of never letting opposing teams browbeat him in any transfer dealings. When Keegan wanted to buy a player his bid went in, usually from his Chief Executive Freddie Fletcher. And that was it. Keegan was never prepared to get involved in any auction. Yet he usually pulled his signings off. Indeed they used to say that United were like the Mounties – because Keegan always got his man.

Paul Kitson was a prime example. Keegan offered Derby County £2.25 million. Derby County tried to hang out for more. Keegan told me that he wasn't prepared to pay a penny more. The word got back to the Midlands. And Keegan got his man. At £2.25 million. Keegan's dealings in the transfer market were fascinating. When he left it was widely reported that he had spent £60 million in his time as manager of Newcastle United. Give a bob or two and this figure is probably right. But what was conveniently overlooked was the fact that Keegan clawed £20 million back in with some astute selling.

Andy Cole was the best example, bought for £1.75 million from Bristol City and sold to Manchester United 20 months later in a deal which Keegan put as being worth £8.25million to United. Then there was Cole's big mate Ruel Fox. He cost £2.25 million when he joined United from Norwich early in February 1994. When Fox was sold to Gerry Francis in October 1995 Spurs had to come up with £4 million.

There were others. Keegan trebled his money on Barry Venison when he was transferred to Galatasaray for £750,000 in the summer of 1995. He doubled his money on Alex Mathie after bringing the Scot down from Morton. Just before he resigned Keegan was criticised for selling Chris Holland and Darren Huckerby although I feel there was more to these transfers than was ever revealed to the fans. Yet Holland, who cost £100,000 from Preston North End, brought £600,000 into the United coffers when Trevor Francis took him to Birmingham City. Keegan again doubled his money on Huckerby after paying Lincoln City £500,000 for him and selling him to Coventry City for £1 million.

There were some bad buys. Funnily enough these came in two little spells, one right at the beginning of Keegan's reign. Darren

McDonough and Peter Garland arrived from Luton Town and Spurs respectively within four days of eachother. Neither was a success. Then at the beginning of the 1994–95 season the ink was hardly dry on Steve Guppy's £150,000 transfer form from Wycombe Wanderers when Jason Drysdale arrived 24 hours later in a £425,000 deal with Watford boss and former United skipper Glenn Roeder. The left winger and the left-back never got anywhere near the United team – they may claim they were never given the chance – but at least Keegan got his money back when they were sold on to Port Vale and Swindon.

Keegan was involved in nearly 80 transfer dealings in his five years at St James's Park but when he left – and only when he left – his critics were quick to point out that not one single youngster had come through the ranks in his time. To be fair, they had a point. In United's 22-man squad on the back of the club programme at the start of the 1996–97 season only teenager striker Paul Brayson had come through from the juniors under Keegan.

There was some criticism aimed at Keegan even before he left over his decision to pull his reserve side out of the Central League last season. Once again this criticism seemed to be justified. Like a lot of other Premiership clubs, United had the use of a non-league ground to play their reserve matches. They were made welcome at the international stadium by the Gateshead chairman John Gibson, just as Manchester United used to pop down the road to Bury's Gigg Lane. This obviously upset a few people at the Central League. So they asked clubs to play six of their home games at their own mother stadium. Manchester United agreed. Newcastle United – or Kevin Keegan – didn't.

Keegan wanted absolutely nothing to stand in the way of United's bid to win the Premiership title in 1996–97. But surely United could have played three reserve matches at St James's Park at the start of the season and another three at the end? In this way, at times of the year when the grounds were firm, there would have been no damage to St James's Park. But Keegan had made his mind up. And when Keegan made up his mind he didn't normally change it. The result was that only those United players actually in the team got any competitive football. The rest were left kicking their heels and it showed, for when the likes of Warren Barton were given their chance in the United first team they looked decidedly ring rusty when they came in. Understandably so.

Pulling his reserve side out of the Central League was one of the worst decisions Keegan made in his managerial career at St James's Park. In all fairness there were not many poor decisions as Keegan proved to be one of the best and bravest managers the game has ever known. How else can you describe his decision to sell Andy Cole? Or paying a world record £15 million for Geordie boy Alan Shearer.

Then there were the incidents involving Lee Clark and John Beresford. Now Clarkie and Bez were two of Keegan's favourites, but this did not stop them from having very public bust-ups with their manager. Keegan was again in the headlines.

It was United's first season in the Premiership when Keegan showed once more that he was going to take no nonsense from his players, even from a player like Lee Clark, whom many people thought Keegan looked upon as a son. Andy Cole had been scoring goals for fun and Clark was the man behind most of them. However, it all went wrong as it usually does when United head down to the south coast to Southampton.

It was Sunday, 24 October, after the game had been put back 24 hours so that it could be beamed out live by Sky Television. Things had started off badly for United when Robert Lee had a goal disallowed – because Cole had strayed offside.

Then when Matthew Le Tissier opened the scoring with a superb effort after 61 minutes, United's nerves began to show. But no one expected what was to come next. Keegan brought off Clark seven minutes later and sent on Alex Mathie as his substitute. But Clark, obviously upset at being brought off, kicked physiotherapist Derek Wright's bag and then began to storm off towards the tunnel. Keegan chased after Clark and dragged him back into the dug-out. After initially only speaking about the incident on Sky Television, Keegan then gagged his players and himself. Yet amazingly a deaf and dumb woman, a Southampton season ticket holder, was able to lip-read every word from her seat in The Dell stands. Her version was that Keegan bellowed at Clark: 'You are out of order, get back into that dug-out.'

To make matters worse. United lost and Clark looked close to tears when he left The Dell. Although he did not get home until 2 a.m. he was still up when I spoke to him at 8.30. He told me he had been told to travel to play for the reserves at Leicester City that night. He was also dropped for the next match for the Coca-Cola Cup-tie with Wimbledon at Selhurst Park two days later – his 21st birthday. Clark certainly came of age after that incident at Southampton, and the incident was probably noted by every Premiership player and manager in the country. As one United player told me, 'There but for the grace of God go I.'

But Beresford obviously forgot all this in the heat of the game against Aston Villa at St James's Park in season 1995–96. United, fighting it out neck and neck with Manchester United for the greatest prize of all – the FA Carling Premiership – looked decidedly shaky early on in their crucial match with Villa. Keegan was off his feet and out of the dug-out like the proverbial yo-yo. The United manager spotted the reasons why. Villa were getting a bit too much space down their right wing. Instructions were immediately bellowed to Beresford on how to put things right. Bez replied, 'That's rubbish, gaffer,' or words to that effect.

Now in the daily thrust and parry with Keegan and Terry McDermott, John Beresford was always at the forefront. But on this occasion he had gone over the mark. He soon knew it. Once again, with the television cameras virtually up his nose, Keegan showed that he wasn't having any of this – just as he had shown Lee Clark a couple of seasons earlier. Even though there were only 25 minutes gone Keegan immediately substituted Beresford and sent on Robbie Elliott. It was another incredibly brave decision by Keegan. And he was right of course. No player should be allowed to publicly back-chat his manager. No matter who he is. Even if it's all in the heat of the moment.

Some managers might have opted out of giving interviews to the media after the game knowing that the Beresford incident was certain to be brought up. But the game had hardly ended when Keegan was in front of the Sky cameras spilling his heart out.

Bez, a super guy, knew he had done wrong. I got the only Beresford interview after the game. He had already been into see Keegan and he could not apologise enough. There were only four matches of the 1995–96 season left. Bez played in none of them and it's a fair bet he had a miserable summer.

To tell the truth, I wondered if Beresford had played his last game for the club. But despite what other problems Keegan may have had I always felt that he was a lot more forgiving in the latter part of his managerial career. The public bust-ups with Beresford and Clark were isolated affairs. In his time at St James's Park both as a player and a manager those who worked with Keegan would have run through a brick wall for him.

Yes, there were rules Keegan wanted obeyed. But they were not exactly Draconian. When Barry Venison walked into that Bournemouth wine bar instead of going to play tenpin bowling with the rest of the United squad, Keegan relieved him of the captaincy. It must have been a difficult decision for Keegan as on the field Venison epitomised everything that is good about being a captain. But this was an isolated incident. Keegan gave the players their freedom. In return they gave him their respect. Every Newcastle player in Keegan's reign knew what he could and could not do.

If there were two things the players knew they were going to get from Keegan the manager, they were honesty and loyalty. They knew they could trust him.

Take Robert Lee. When Lee joined United from Charlton in September 1992 he brought John Hollins, the former Chelsea and England midfielder and a respected figure in the game, along as his representative. Yet when the time came to renegotiate a new contract there was no Hollins. Nor anyone else for that matter. Lee was happy to let Keegan sort out all the financial aspects of his new deal. I remember the Cockney telling me he had no worries at all at letting Keegan handle what was probably the most important part of the transaction. It must be one of the few transfers in the game in which the player was happy to put himself in the hands of someone who technically was on the other side of the fence.

Keegan had so many qualities as a manager. Of course it helped that he had been there as a player, seen it all and done it all himself. His reputation was spread over the whole world. That is, it appears, everywhere but Taiwan. I still have a little chuckle when I remember the time we had to stop over in Taiwan on our way from Singapore to Osaka in Japan in the summer Far East tour. We all piled off our jumbo jet for an hour in Taiwan. Now I've been all over the world with Kevin Keegan and to every part of this country. Wherever he has gone he has been surrounded by people wanting to touch or talk to one of the most popular guys this country has ever known. But Taiwan? That was different. Obviously the people there hadn't a clue who he was. There he stood in splendid isolation, on his own without anyone else near him in Taiwan airport. Almost like a little boy lost. Even the public address system announcer was confused, telling the United party: 'Would the England team please now board their plane?'

One plane Keegan did not manage to reach was the tactical plane. His critics were always trying to say he was tactically naïve. My answer was always the same – look at the league table. Yes, Keegan did not have United spending hours in training practising corners and free-kicks. He preferred to let the players play. He wanted United to win from open play. Not from a corner kick or free kick. That's why he always bought players who were comfortable on the ball. Even his central defenders, Philippe Albert and Darren Peacock, were happy with the ball at their feet. Then Keegan once told me: 'We don't buy defenders who can defend well and nothing else. We buy defenders who can play.'

Keegan admitted that he was surprised at just how much work there is in being a manager. Mind you, he never helped himself by putting himself through a punishing schedule that only a man as fit as he is could endure. When I used to go to Durham on a daily basis I was worn out just watching Keegan. He was always the first to arrive at the club's Maiden Castle training headquarters, and for starters he would take on either physio Paul Ferrisor or striker Paul Kitson at squash. I say squash, but it was more like World War Three. Keegan obviously was the boss and if anything this only made Ferris and Kitson more determined to beat him. So when you take into consideration Keegan's loathing of losing no matter what the sport or competition, we all used to stand and wait for them to drag themselves off the court.

It was only in his later days that Keegan used to stop for breath before conducting the evening paper and radio press conferences. Then he was off again in search of his favourite pastime – his beloved head tennis with his trusty partner Terry MacDermott. The fact that there was always a tenner up for grabs as a little side bet meant that come hell or high water there was usually only one winning team – the manager and his assistant.

By now there was the little matter of the whole point of the day, training the players of Newcastle United. Now the term track-suit manager could have been invented for Kevin Keegan, for while the younger Terry Mac was content to coach from the touchlines Keegan led from the front and was always in the thick of things. He rarely missed the full-scale practice matches and even the fastest men on the books like Steve Howey and John Beresford knew that they would have to be on their mettle to shake off the gritty little so-and-so with the greying hair who never knew when he was beaten in the sprints.

After training Keegan had to face the national press and then more often than not it was up to St James's Park to catch up with his administration work in his office. I know that when I called in to pick my car up after a day in the office the bay with the sign 'Kevin Keegan manager' was still usually occupied at tea-time. And I for one would not attempt to hazard a guess where Keegan and Terry Mac headed off to in their relentless pursuit for players in the bid to make United top of the pile.

'Everyone from the chairman downwards at this club works way above the demands of their contracts,' Keegan once told me. Explaining why he never shirked his mundane administrative tasks Keegan added: 'You have to do all the paperwork and sit in on the meetings otherwise someone else is controlling your life.' Now someone controlling his life is the worst thing imaginable for Keegan for if anyone is in control of his own destiny then that man is Kevin Keegan. He soon found out that life as a manager was so different from life as a footballer. After he had spent exactly 12 months in the hot-seat at St James's Park he pointed out to me: 'As a player, I didn't realise what an easy life I had compared with a manager. You just have to keep yourself fit and make sure you live up to expectations. As a player everything is done for you. You just turn up and the kit is all laid out in the dressing-room.

'But there is such a large part of a soccer club you don't see as a player which is the part that makes the club tick. As a player you can hide behind people. As a manager you cannot hide behind anyone.

'I quite enjoy all the aspects of being a manager, even the paperwork. I love winning games of football. It makes your weekend. Losing makes you want to get back on Monday to start all over again.

'But the hardest part of the job is undoubtedly telling a player he is not playing when in your heart you know he should be.'

But Keegan knew only too well how important it was to tell a player he was leaving him out before the side was announced publicly after the way he was left out of the England side in 1982 by Bobby Robson and did not know until he was told by a member of the press. 'However stupid your reasons might seem to the player you have to tell him yourself,' he said.

Although Keegan was a media man's dream until the latter stages of his reign, he admitted that one of the most vital lessons he learned as a manager was making sure you do not give anything away which could help to motivate the opposition. He told me: 'The best lesson of that was in 1974 when Super Mac was shouting his mouth off in the papers about all Liverpool's weaknesses in the week before Newcastle played us in the FA Cup final at Wembley and all Bill Shankly had to do was to stick the cuttings up on the dressing-room wall.'

There was one way Keegan was different from any other United manager I have known. I often had friendly little chats with Arthur Cox in his office at St James's Park in his days as United manager. It wasn't that Arthur saw me as someone special, but he loves football so much he would talk to anyone about it. Then came Jack Charlton and life changed dramatically for me. For big Jack often involved me in transfer talks with coach Willie McFaul, his number two Maurice Setters and youth development officer Peter Kirkley. Willie McFaul was a friend, apart from when he invited me into his office for one of my regular dressing-downs, usually after I had revealed one of his transfer targets. Jim Smith was an even bigger friend, and most of the time I spent in his office was planning our social lives on a Friday night. Then came Ossie Ardiles. Now Ossie always welcomed the press into his office for drinks. I just wish I had understood what he was saying in the two years I worked alongside him.

And Keegan? Well, as far as I know no one ever got into Keegan's office. I did – only once, although I cannot remember why I was honoured. But my beady eyes darted all over the place like there was no tomorrow. My lasting impression was of a huge picture of Bill Shankly, Keegan's Liverpool manager and possibly the man he respected most of all. There was also a giant but unopened bottle of whisky – a Manager of the Month award – standing in the corner.

I always regarded the closed office door policy by Keegan as signifying he did not want any of the press to get too close to him. He certainly had no favourites among the press. Even *The Sun* with whom he had a contract for a regular column received no favours or tip-offs from Keegan in the day-to-day activities at the club.

As befitting someone who set himself high standards it's no surprise that his demands on the people who worked closely with him were high. Some didn't last the pace. Youth development officer Peter Kirkley moved down the coast to Middlesbrough. Youth team coach Colin Suggett switched to Ipswich. Fans' favourite John Anderson drifted out of the game after a spell as reserve team manager until he got back in, working with Radio Newcastle. Kitman Chris Guthrie, an England angling international, left and no doubt became an even better angler.

When Keegan's managerial career is put under the microscope in years to come one thing will not be in doubt: he brought some of the best and most exciting players to St James's Park. They don't come any better than Alan Shearer. Or David Ginola. And what about Tino Asprilla? But none of these megastars were as big as Keegan himself.

I got a first-hand view of this when I decided to pop down to United's training ground at Durham to see Asprilla's first training session. I wasn't surprised at what I saw. But it's a fair guess the Colombian was. For a number of reasons.

First, there were hordes of fans who turned up for their first real glimpse of Asprilla. They saw Asprilla take part in a full-scale practice match. There was a little fellow in the same team as

United's new £7.5 million signing, a little fellow who was beginning to go grey at the temples – Keegan. But despite this he was probably the best player on the field as he put everything into it. I never found out just what Asprilla thought of his 45-year-old manager taking a full part in the practice match.

But this wasn't all. Understandably there was a huge queue to get Asprilla's autograph. If Tino had taken the trouble to look up, he would have seen that the queue for Keegan's prized signature was twice as long. No matter who Keegan signed – and he signed the best – he was always the biggest name at the club.

Most of Keegan's strengths as a manager have been well documented. But one that the supporters were probably unaware of was the fact he never bleated about injuries or suspensions – something which all his predecessors I worked with moaned about most of the time. He took injuries and suspensions in his stride. It wasn't that he did not care but just that he knew there was nothing he could do about it. Quite often when one of his key players was having a fitness test Keegan was conspicuous by his absence. He was either on the squash court, or more likely playing head tennis with his trusty partner Terry McDermott. I could never fathom out how Keegan always managed to partner Terry Mac in what was supposed to be an open draw. Or how the pair of them were perennial head tennis champions.

Unfortunately – and it will be something he will always regret – Keegan was unable to make Newcastle United the champions of his country. Indeed I don't think he will make anyone champions, for I am convinced that Kevin Keegan will never manage another football club in this country.

So what would he like on his epitaph? Kevin Keegan, a player who went on to be a great manager? Or Kevin Keegan, a manager who was a great player? I think both are correct.

# 13

## PRESS-GANGED

KEVIN KEEGAN WAS easily the best manager I have ever worked with press-wise. But in some ways he was also the worst. I found him a real Jekyll and Hyde character to deal with. Life was a roller-coaster. One moment you were up. The next moment you were down.

You knew you were all right on a morning when he said 'Morning girls'. But things weren't so good when you got a 'What do you lot want?'. Yet in all the times I travelled down to United's training ground at Durham he only failed me once. That was when he got tied up with a top quality Sunday newspaper and was not available before a match with Leicester City. Peter Beardsley, who had fractured his cheekbone in the game at Filbert Street, saved my bacon with a 'It wasn't your fault' message to the Leicester player.

But fall-outs between pressmen and football managers are inevitable. They are an occupational hazard. Especially for local evening paper men who are always quite close to their respective club. However, falling out with Keegan and falling out with a mere mortal manager were two completely different things. In my view it is fair to say that Keegan ruled the press with fear – fear that if you upset him you were out in the cold. Without going into the rights and wrongs of the situation, perhaps the press made a rod for its own back over the Tim Taylor affair.

Taylor, an experienced sports writer, had been brought in to look after the affairs of United for our sister paper *The Journal*. Yet in his first season Taylor was banned by Keegan, as was his paper. *The Journal* eventually had their status restored. But the ban on Taylor stayed. In the end Taylor was finally switched to the less important job of covering Sunderland. In effect Taylor's livelihood was threatened despite several appeals to Keegan. With hindsight perhaps it would have been in the interests of the other press to close ranks and tell Keegan this just was not on, but nobody dared confront him.

Certainly working daily with Keegan was like sitting on a powder keg. You knew you could not afford to cross him or you were out. There were occasions when Keegan felt I had crossed him and he made my working life a misery. After one particularly bad blasting I even tried to quit my job.

Yet for most of the time Keegan was a dream to deal with. The words came tumbling out his mouth like gold-dust. After a match he could satisfy the Sunday papers, the morning papers, television and radio. He had this knack of coming up with different words to describe the same match to all the different sections of the media. And how we loved him. Throw in the fact that he was completely honest with us – and brave – then it was easy to see why the media men queued up to see him. There was none of this 'We're taking every game as it comes' stuff managers troll out. Keegan said it as it was. He never shirked an issue. Until the last few months of his reign.

I particularly remember his press conference at Highbury after Arsenal had dumped United out of the Coca-Cola Cup in January 1996. Everything that could go wrong for United and Keegan that night did. Lee Dixon kicked lumps out of David Ginola yet it was the Frenchman who was sent off. There was also a very public bust-up between his number two Terry McDermott and Arsenal boss Bruce Rioch. On top of this United lost.

But that wasn't all. It was the day Terry Venables announced he had decided to quit the England job in the summer after Euro 96. Keegan was the people's choice. Everyone wanted to talk to him.

Suddenly I was surrounded by the London press boys. Would Keegan do a press conference? They did not think he would especially as he had a little brush live on Independent Television. But he did. I was at just about every press conference Keegan did. This was the best. Now the London mafia can be hostile to opposing managers, yet Keegan had them eating out of his hands. It all ended in laughter. A rather flustered young female television reporter pleaded with Keegan to meet her in the car park because she had been separated from her camera crew. 'That's the best offer I've had all night,' quipped Keegan. He had done it again.

There were stacks of laughs on the way. Keegan was so good that I used to go to Durham without the security of a back-up story. But with a ten o'clock deadline for our first edition there were some scary moments. We were never allowed into any inner sanctum but usually he talked to us in the corridor beside the radiators and the public telephone.

As the deadline rapidly approached one day I became more and more worried as there was no sign of him. To save time I dialled my copytaker, Linzi Copeland, and asked her to set herself up for my copy. I left the phone dangling. Keegan duly appeared and as usual came up with the goods. But then he spotted the dangling phone and before I could get on it he spent five minutes making small talk to Linzi as I fretted and the lads on the sports desk panicked. I thought the rest of the press lads were going to die laughing. This was the Keegan I loved and will remember in years to come.

Loved? Well, how else can I describe the way I felt when Keegan gave me that world exclusive that he had signed Alan Shearer out in Bangkok? Or the host of other exclusives he dropped in my lap?

But there had to be a price to pay for all this – and there was. My fall-outs with Keegan were almost legendary in the press world. I can laugh at the very first fall-out now because of the way he strung me along. It was a story I shared with Mick Lowes when the big man was working for Radio Newcastle. It all concerned the amount of money Keegan had to spend and big Mick had it all on tape. Anyway, when I phoned United's training ground Terry Mac said Keegan was annoyed with me and that no one was talking to me. That day we all travelled to Bristol – only on one occasion for a game when they flew to Cambridge did

Keegan let me travel with the team for a game in this country and even that was a bit of a misunderstanding – for the match with City at Ashton Gate the following day.

At night in a Bristol hotel there was none of the usual banter from Keegan and United directed at the travelling press boys. There was only one thing for it. I would have to confront the man himself. So at breakfast time I presented myself at the door to the restaurant. I approached coach Derek Fazackerley to see if Keegan would talk to me.

'There's a journalist to see you gaffer,' said Faz.

'I don't see a journalist, only Alan Oliver,' was Keegan's reply. It was vintage Keegan and the United players nearly choked on their cornflakes with laughter. Keegan kept me waiting and as he left the restaurant he walked straight past me. My heart sank into my boots, but suddenly he was there in front of me. To this day I don't know whether he was playing a game with me or whether he came back after seeing the pathetic look on my face, but I got a pep talk from Keegan. He made me feel as though I would run through that brick wall for him.

The United players always told me that I should be honoured because in a way he treated me like he treated them and that he wanted the same response from me as he got from them. But all the managers I have worked with have been the same in that they have conveniently forgotton that my first loyalty is to the *Evening Chronicle* and its readers.

I remember once getting a 'We're-all-in-this-together' speech from Ossie Ardiles and telling him I could not recall picking my wages up from St James's Park. In a way Keegan was the same. He always kept the press at arm's length but he seemed to want more from the local guys, and despite all our bust-ups I can say hand on heart that at no time did I hate him or anything like that. When we were back on speaking terms again it was all as though nothing had happened from his point of view.

But two bust-ups left me really down. And nearly out. After some minor skirmishes the first came in United's first Premiership season. Early in February United were knocked out of the FA Cup by Luton Town after a replay at Kenilworth Road on the Wednesday night. After the match the whole party headed for Bournemouth for a break before their game with Wimbledon on the Saturday. Keegan agreed to make himself available to the local press over the phone back in Newcastle if we did not go to Bournemouth and we did not beef at this.

On the Friday morning I took a call from a fellow journalist saying that there had been a bit of bother down in Bournemouth with three players, skipper Barry Venison, Steve Howey and Alex Mathie, spending time in a wine bar when they should have been ten-pin bowling with the rest of the squad. It was bad enough for Keegan to threaten to send them home and Venison was relieved of the captaincy the following day.

I couldn't get through to Keegan in Bournemouth, but then I heard that the story was going to be blown across the Saturday morning papers. At this stage the *Evening Chronicle* was not going to run the story. I rang the club and said that all hell was going to break loose the next morning. The result was that the club issued an official statement and immediately the *Chronicle* was off into action again with a front-page lead story.

I honestly thought Keegan had sanctioned the statement but I soon found out otherwise when he rang me from Bournemouth with the mother and father of all rockets. It was soon made clear that I wasn't going to be made welcome at the training ground. I received a letter from Venison's solicitor. The only complaint was that I had said the incident happened on the Thursday night when in fact it had occurred on the afternoon.

The morning papers went bonkers the following day. One even carried the headline 'PLONKERS'. But I was the only one banned by Keegan, and all I was guilty of was reporting on a club statement. Even my colleague on the *Sunderland Echo,* Graham Robinson, who carried the story at the same time was not banned. And there was no action against Metro Radio who put it out as the *Evening Chronicle* hit the street. It was business as usual as well for the North-East's national newspaper men who had had a field day with the story.

Despite our fall-outs Keegan always insisted he liked me personally although he obviously did not always like what I wrote and he never asked the directors to ban me from my seat in the press box. But he refused to talk or see me for the rest of that season. That was from the middle of February. There was no hint from him whether or not normal service was going to be resumed the following season. I didn't know how I stood until I went to Wrexham for Dixie McNeil's testimonial on 1 August. There were no handshakes. No recriminations. No finger-pointing and the matter was not even discussed. I stood at the back of his post-match press conference and when the morning papers had finished I just kept on talking. It was over. The previous incident was never discussed between us, but I sunk a few beers on the way home from North Wales that night.

The next bust-up didn't last as long, though I was left so shaken by it all I tried to quit. It came just after the sale of Andy Cole. At the time there were all sorts of stories flying around about United. By now the club had become big, big news and it was well known that the Sunday papers were watching the United players when they relaxed and had a few drinks in one of the town's many clubs.

A reporter from our news team went to a player's home and tried to clear up the situation. Now if there is anything a football writer hates it's the news side involving themselves in situations like this. He's always on a loser when this happens, though they have their jobs to do. So what happened had absolutely nothing to do with me and I forgot all about it.

That's why I was taken by surprise at the absolute ferocity of Keegan's attack on me in the corridor behind the press room after the Manchester United game in the middle of January 1995.

I protested my innocence but Keegan did not want to listen. He told me I was guilty until I could prove my innocence. Looking back I know I had taken all the backlash and frustrations Keegan had felt at the Cole deal. I was absolutely shattered. I went to work the next day and did my stuff. But I told my sports editor Paul New I couldn't take any more and that I wanted to quit. I refused to go to the FA Cup replay with Blackburn on the Wednesday night.

Fortunately Paul New bumped into Keegan socially at St James's Park the following day and tried to straighten things out, though it wasn't until the last minute that I decided to go to Hillsborough for United's match with Sheffield Wednesday on the Saturday. I'm glad I did. When Keegan spotted me he stopped his press conference and singled me out. I knew then that everything was going to be okay.

But my troubles for the day weren't over. I had suffered mentally and I knew I looked terrible. As I walked away from Keegan I bumped into a United player – he's no longer at the club – who told me how awful I looked and that he hoped I was dying. The trouble was that he meant it. It wasn't very nice for me, especially as it was all witnessed by a handful of fans. I didn't care. All that mattered to me was that I was back on speaking terms with Kevin Keegan. He was always the most important person at the club to me while he was there.

After this there were plenty of other disagreements but there were no more real bust-ups. Keegan used to have his say. I had mine as the players dived for cover. When they felt it was safe to put their heads above the parapet the players all asked, 'What was that about then?'

I did get into trouble again with Keegan in the 1995–96 season over Tino Asprilla. Quite frankly some of the stuff dished out on Asprilla from the nationals was disgraceful. He received publicity Attila the Hun would have been proud of. I kept out of it yet I still managed to upset KK and chairman Sir John Hall. I tried to say that while Keegan had never moved an inch on his desire to sign Asprilla the board were wavering. United took it that I was saying that there was a power struggle going on between Keegan and the board when in fact I was trying to say the opposite. But when you get it in the neck from the two most popular and powerful men in the region in Keegan and Sir John, you have to have a skin as tough as a rhinoceros. However, I was determined not to be banned again and to tell the truth I think Keegan was weary of fighting with me.

On the Saturday night before the Manchester United game last season Sky Television flew me down to Heathrow to appear on their *Hold The Back Page* discussion programme. I waxed lyrical about Keegan. It came from the heart, but I knew it would cut no ice with him in our latest little dispute. The following morning I went straight from Newcastle airport to United's training ground at Durham for the pre-match press conference. He tried to tell me I was banned but with hordes of kids milling around him preparing to play their sport – Sunday was a busy day at United's university-owned training ground – he simply sat on the stairs and everything was sorted out.

The days of being banned were clearly now over. Our last little disagreement was over something I had written about his decision to scrap his reserve team when we were at the Player of the Month awards won by Philippe Albert just before Christmas. Keegan made his point – forcibly as usual – but then ended it all by saying 'Let's talk about Philippe'.

It's a pity that things weren't the same press-wise with Keegan in the last six months as they had been earlier. He was usually so fair with everyone. I remember sitting having dinner in our hotel high up in the hills of Tuscany – our only neighbours were the Trappist monks – before the Anglo-Italian Cup tie with Lucchese in the November of the promotion season. Keegan and his United backroom staff were on the next table and as usual the banter was great. But for some reason the United coaches decided I should buy them a bottle of wine. Derek Fazackerley was particularly insistent. There was only one thing for it. I would have to buy a bottle of wine out of my meagre allowance for the trip. But Keegan wasn't having any of this. He stepped in and put a stop to all this nonsense!

One day the press guys will never forget during the build-up to season 1995–96 was when he invited us all down to the club's training ground at Maiden Castle and put us through our paces. He had already gone through his usual daily routine – squash, local press, head tennis, training and national press – when in the afternoon he gave two dozen of the media a two-hour training session. He even arranged through the club's sponsors Adidas for all of us to wear the famous Predator boots.

He had Terry Mac and Derek Fazackerley with him; Keith Gillespie and Warren Barton were the two players told by Keegan to stay behind and give up their afternoon. I could not help thinking at the time that the two players must have been bored out of their minds. But for two hours Keegan patiently gave us the sort of training session he usually saved for his players. He was absolutely superb. I left Durham that day appreciating just why the United players were prepared to sweat blood for him.

Yet, as I've already said, in the main I believe it is fair to say that Keegan ruled the press by fear. His press conferences were so good that no one dare risk being banned. The fear factor was certainly in evidence when I discovered by chance that Les

Ferdinand had broken his toe before the end of the 1995–96 season.

Now United made it clear that they did not want this news to leak out, especially to opposing teams who would surely have tried to have taken advantage, and I played ball. But I hinted to Keegan that because of this I should be given the story when it broke. Well, after the Southampton game at St James's Park on 17 April United had a ten-day break because of England's commitments and I knew that it would all come out.

I was horrified when he told the morning paper guys. I felt he should have kept it for me to use the following night. To make matters worse, he announced to the packed press conference that I was the only reporter who had known about Ferdie's toe injury and that I had been afraid to use the story with the threat of him not speaking to me. I suppose it was his way of keeping me in my place but I felt as though Keegan had let me down.

I wasn't the only one. On the day when it was rumoured that Lee Clark had asked for a transfer, I watched one of the guys from Metro Radio ask Keegan if he could broach the subject before he began his interview with the manager. He was told in no uncertain terms that he could not. Then Keegan went into the morning paper press conference and spilled the beans on the Clark affair.

When Keegan resigned there were the odd rumblings that he had been helped on his way by the press. The misinformed fans who were saying this simply did not know what they were talking about. I bet that every single member of the press corps wanted Keegan to stay, even though he turned United from the most open club in the country to one where he only gave press conferences immediately before and immediately after a game. Yet one Keegan press conference was as good as ten from a normal manager. We all knew that whoever came in to replace Keegan would not be in the same class. No one press-wise suffered under Keegan more than I did. But despite all this I have never worked with a manager as good as Kevin Keegan. I know I never will.

# 14

## KEEGAN THE MAN

KEVIN KEEGAN HAS always been his own man. Frank Sinatra's *My Way* could easily have been penned for him. All that Keegan has achieved in life has been done his way. I have rarely met anyone as strong, both physically and mentally. His principles are so strong they are almost overbearing, and there is never any way Keegan is ever going to let himself be compromised.

He has never been afraid of speaking his mind. He once told me, 'I have never seen speaking your mind as a risk. You cannot live your life working out what other people think you should do. You might make a mistake but you must live or die by your own decisions.' Certainly no one can ever accuse Kevin Keegan of not making his own decisions.

Yet at the same time he was a bundle of laughs, especially when Terry McDermott was around, which was most of the time. The pair of them were rascals. Real wind-up merchants. But you always knew how far you could go with them. Lee Clark and John Beresford went too far and paid the penalty. When it came to football, then they were always deadly serious.

I think it's fair to say that Keegan was also unpredictable, someone who was always capable of doing the unexpected. Neil Harman and Steve Curry were two national newspaper men based in London with the *Daily Mail* and *Daily Express* respectively, but because Keegan had made United big news they spent a lot of time on Tyneside. After one Wednesday night game they had time on their hands before the Saturday, so they decided to ask Keegan to lunch the following day. To their surprise Keegan accepted and a lunch was arranged on Teesside near the Keegan family home at Wynyard.

Now I can honestly say I've never even seen Kevin Keegan with a glass in his hand but another legend was born on that day. Several bottles of Australian Chardonnay were ordered to wash down the Dover sole and, as they say, enough was put away to sink the *Titanic*. Then the karaoke started. The story goes that Keegan needed no help from Frank Sinatra as he belted out what could be his theme tune of *My Way*. This was a rare occasion of Keegan letting his hair down in public.

Amazingly for someone who has never been out of the public eye since he was a teenager, Keegan insisted on his privacy. He protects it, and anyone who invades it is not welcome. One photographer took the trouble of hiring a light plane and flying to Teesside where he took the first aerial shots of Keegan's new £1 million palatial five-bedroomed house, which includes swimming pool, gymnasium, conservatory, and a complex of nine stables and courtyard. And what did the photographer get for his trouble? A little ban on him attending games at St James's Park. Keegan is essentially a family man but any talk of his family was strictly taboo. In the near five years he spent as United's manager, I could not name his two daughters.

Certainly, while Keegan could never walk through the centre of Newcastle because he would have stopped the traffic, his daughters would hardly have been recognised. I recognised them one day but only because they were with Kevin's wife Jean, bounding up the stairs at St James's Park before a game with Nottingham Forest. Now the Keegan girls had arrived at exactly the same time as the Forest team bus. They were caught up in it all to such an extent they were nearly swept into the visiting dressing-room by the Forest players. The three girls giggled their heads off at this. I saw it all, and initially I thought it would make a good piece for my Saturday night 'behind the scenes' column. But I knew Kevin would not have been happy at involving his family, so I forgot all about it.

What I will never forget is the way Keegan devoted himself to cheering up the youngsters on Tyneside and especially those who had a disability. The way he devoted himself to making them happy often brought a tear to my eye. But more important, looking in the eyes of the youngsters told it all. They simply adored him. He insisted that there was no publicity given to the vast majority of his charity work. He would often turn up at hospitals unannounced with a couple of United players. He is never happier than when he is knee deep in youngsters.

A couple of weeks before he resigned, Keegan, Jean, Terry McDermott, and his Chairman Sir John Hall, took a couple of hundred kids to Lapland. Colleagues who were on the trip told me they have never seen Kevin more relaxed. My last social engagement with Keegan was at the Newcastle Breweries-*Evening Chronicle* Player of the Month awards, just before Christmas. Keegan and Alistair Wilson (Chairman of the Breweries) loved to invite handicapped youngsters along to meet the players and celebrities. On this occasion the youngsters were from the Percy Hedley Special School. When Keegan walked in every face lit up. Keegan loved to mingle among the youngsters. He spotted one youngster in a wheelchair, 14-year-old Andrew Fawcus from Newbiggin-on-Sea, and playfully told him off for wearing a United top which was out of date. Keegan then whipped off his own top and pulled it over the head of the delighted youngster.

Even at The Valley in what was to be his last game in charge of Newcastle United in the FA Cup replay with Charlton, Keegan never forgot the common touch, which made him the man he is. United's mascot for the game was a little seven-year-old girl who was understandably thrilled at the prospect of the most exciting day in her life so far. But somehow there was a breakdown in communication and the girl, called Stephanie, was left alone and bewildered in the unfriendly corridors outside the dressing-room. Quite naturally Stephanie was upset and she sobbed her heart out as the United players headed back into their dressing-room, after warming up on one of the coldest days I have ever watched a football match. That's when she was spotted by Keegan. When he realised who she was Keegan could not get her into the dressing-room quickly enough to meet her heroes. A United team picture appeared from almost nowhere and Keegan made sure each and every one of his players signed it before he presented it to her. Once again Keegan took off his own track-suit top and gave it to little Stephanie. He then made sure she was at the mascot's rightful place at the head of the team as they went out to do battle with Charlton. Her little face was a picture of joy. As in the case with Andrew Fawcus, Keegan did not know that his kindly deed had been witnessed.

Like any other parent, he is aware of the evil of drugs. That's why Newcastle played a combined Gateshead-Blyth match at the start of this season. The £45,000 raised went to help fight drug abuse in Blyth.

This is one story the public knew about. But for every one they heard, there were dozens that never came to light. There was a particularly poignant visit for Keegan where he unveiled a memorial to the 168 men and boys killed in Stanley in a pit explosion in 1909. Keegan's grandfather Frank had helped save the lives of 28 fellow miners. There's no doubt in my mind that Frank Keegan's bravery had been passed down through the years. If I was in the trenches I could not think of anyone better to have beside me than Kevin Keegan. His loyalty knows no bounds. He is incredibly loyal to those who are loyal to him, like his backroom staff and pals Terry McDermott and Arthur Cox, and to his players. And loyal to those who have helped him.

Alistair Wilson was the driving force behind Newcastle Breweries when Keegan was a player at St James's Park. The Breweries actually sponsored Keegan's time as a Newcastle player, and if it wasn't for them it's doubtful whether he would have ever arrived on Tyneside in the first place. Keegan has never forgotten this. That's why the attendance at the Newcastle Breweries-*Evening Chronicle* Player of the Month awards was nearly always 100 per cent by the United players.

I remember one occasion when Tino Asprilla was conspicious by his absence. The Colombian found himself berated the following day by Terry McDermott. Asprilla does not understand much English, but he got the message when Terry Mac simply said, 'Tino. Brewery?'

Keegan wasn't short of a bob or two, but not once has he let his riches go to his head. Almost a teetotaller, he nevertheless loved being the first at the bar to buy a round of drinks. His working-class origins meant that his feet have never strayed far from the ground. I've never known a man so ego-free. Nobody wears his heart on his sleeve in the same way as Keegan. Keegan counts the Sultan of Brunei as one of his personal friends. Yet he is never more comfortable than when he is mixing with his own. He never forgot the ordinary people. His epitaph could easily read, 'Kevin Keegan, Man of the People'. But he was also a man of moods and I was on the wrong end of one of these moods more often than I would have wanted.

In the time I have known Keegan and worked with him, I have never seen him refuse to sign an autograph. Little old ladies who interrupted his dinner in some hotel. John, who seems to wait permanently outside St James's Park. And Keith, who never misses a United game. These last two must have Keegan's autograph hundreds of times. He would know that. But he still always signed. Considering his time as a player and a manager, and his popularity, Kevin must have signed more autographs than anyone in history.

After his family and football, Keegan's other passion is horses. He's involved with one of his big pals and former England, Southampton and United colleague, Mick Channon, in breeding and training horses. He once said he'd like to take part in the Grand National. I, for one, would not bet against it. It would be a challenge and Kevin Keegan loves nothing more than a challenge.

That's why he is such a talented man. That and hard work. He is fluent in German, and at Villa Park last season he conducted a whole interview with a radio guy from Germany in that language. Keegan also has a way with words from his own country. That's why he is in such demand as an after-dinner speaker. But he could never bring himself to charge them the going rate for a name such as his.

Someone who would never make an after-dinner speaker is Arthur Cox, the man who, with Stan Seymour, first brought Keegan to Newcastle United. Cox has always been a man of few words. But when he does speak, the words are always measured and worth listening to. With Terry McDermott, Arthur Cox probably knows Keegan better than any other man. Cox described Keegan as the best person he knows and someone who has never short-changed anyone in his life.

Terry McDermott simply calls Keegan one of the greatest men the game of football has ever known. Yet it all started in such humble surroundings – typical of the times Keegan was born into. Kevin's dad, Joe, was a miner who moved from his home town of Hutton-le-Hole to find work in the Yorkshire pits. Those miners were a different breed, tough as the boots they had to wear to go down the mines. There is no doubt some of Joe Keegan's toughness rubbed off on his son. Joe was determined that his son was never going to follow him down the mines. Kevin was equally determined to be a footballer. But he was a bit on the short side, and set about making sure that he was at least strong enough to stand up to the rigours of football by tossing weights around the family home in Yorkshire.

That's when Keegan's character started to emerge. Strong. Honest. Loyal. Charismatic. Caring. Inspirational. His attitude to life has always been 'There's a big wide world out there with plenty of opportunities'. Kevin Keegan took that world. By storm.

# 15

## LIFE AFTER KEEGAN

THE DAYS AFTER KEEGAN quit were unreal on Tyneside. After the initial two sentence quotes from Keegan and the United board, silence again reigned supreme at St James's Park.

The big question was just who could ever replace the void left by Keegan? Keegan himself would have been fascinated by the names put forward as his successor. For he had links with the three main ones.

*Kenny Dalglish*: It was Dalglish who was called down from Celtic and Scotland to replace Keegan when he left Liverpool and headed off to Hamburg and Germany in 1977.

*Bobby Robson*: Robson had been Keegan's team manager in his final days as an England player. But Keegan was furious with Robson, not for ending his England career in 1982 but for not telling him to his face. Keegan actually found out from the *Evening Chronicle*.

*John Toshack*: Keegan and Toshack had formed a successful Little and Large partnership in their glory days at Liverpool.

Before there was any official news of Keegan's replacement Terry McDermott and Arthur Cox were given the job of raising United's morale in what was always going to be a difficult game against Aston Villa at Villa Park. The fans were down and some were so distraught they handed their tickets over to their pals because they could not bear to watch a United without Keegan. One United banner at Villa Park summed it all up. It simply said: 'Thanks for the memories, Kev.'

Terry McDermott and Cox did a superb job lifting United at Villa Park. When Villa keeper Mark Bosnich slipped and presented Lee Clark with United's second goal, Terry Mac quipped, 'It was Kevin who tripped him.' After the game – it ended in a 2–2 draw – all the talk was that it had been a performance so typical of those under Keegan. The name of the former United manager was on everybody's lips.

United knew they had to act fast to get a new manager and after Robson appeared to be the favourite, Kenny Dalglish was installed in the hot-seat on 14 January 1997, six days after Keegan quit and the night before the FA Cup replay with Charlton Athletic at St James's Park. Ironically, as soon as Dalglish was installed Bobby Robson hit trouble with a capital T with the Catalan fans at Barcelona and then John Toshack parted company with Spanish club Deportivo of Coruna.

Dalglish was given a typical Geordie welcome both on the night of his appointment and before the replay with Charlton Athletic. But there was no chanting of his name until the game at the end of February. The strains of *Keegan's Wonderland* sung so often and with such gusto seemed to hang in the air.

It's not as if no one appreciated Dalglish and what he has achieved in the game. Everyone agreed that he was the best man to take over from Keegan. When he scored that dramatic late hat-trick against Leicester City early in February, Alan Shearer dedicated it to Keegan. After the same match Dalglish said that if United won anything it would be down to Keegan.

Yet Keegan had been the first to say that life must go on at St James's Park without him.

Exactly a year before Keegan went, I had talked to Terry McDermott about their four years together at United. When I asked him what the situation would be if Keegan ever left, he replied that he would be out of the door with him as if they were tied together by a piece of string. However, Keegan insisted that McDermott stayed, and of course McDermott was right to stay. While he is there a part of Kevin Keegan will always be there and this is not a problem to Dalglish.

No one will be wanting United to succeed under Dalglish and

McDermott more than Keegan. It must not be forgotten that Keegan spent seven years on Tyneside – two as a player and nearly five as a manager. That's longer than he has stayed anywhere in his professional career. Kevin Keegan will always be a part of Newcastle United. He may have gone. But he will never be forgotten.

# THE GREAT CAREER

1951: Born Armthorpe, Yorkshire, 14 February
1968: Joined Scunthorpe United as apprentice
1971: Moved to Liverpool for £35,000
1972: England debut v Wales in Cardiff
1977: Transferred to SV Hamburg for £500,000
1980: Joined Southampton for £420,000
1982: Last England game as substitute v Spain in Madrid, World Cup. Won 63 caps, scored 21 goals. Transferred to Newcastle for £100,000.
1984: Retired from playing
1992: Returned to soccer in February as manager of Newcastle and three months later signed a three-year contract
1993: Newcastle promoted to Premiership as Division One champions
1994: Keegan made a Director of Football and signed a deal to stay ten years
1996: Newcastle finished runners-up to Manchester United in the Premiership. Keegan broke world transfer record by paying Blackburn £15 million for England striker Alan Shearer.
1997: Resigned as manager of Newcastle on 8 January

# HONOURS

| | |
|---|---|
| League Championship winner: | 1972-73, 1975-76, 1976-77 |
| FA Cup winner: | 1974 |
| European Cup winner: | 1977 |
| UEFA Cup winner: | 1973, 1976 |
| Footballer of the Year: | 1975-76 |
| European Footballer of the Year: | 1977–78, 1978–79 |
| PFA Player of the Year | 1981–82 |
| Division One Manager of the Season: | 1992-93 |

# LEAGUE RECORD

## LEAGUE RECORD AT NEWCASTLE

|            |             | P   | W   | D  | L  | F   | A   | Pts |
|------------|-------------|-----|-----|----|----|-----|-----|-----|
| Feb 1992:  | Div One     | 16  | 7   | 2  | 7  | 22  | 25  | 23  |
| 1992-93:   | Div One     | 46  | 29  | 9  | 8  | 85  | 37  | 96  |
| 1993-94:   | Premiership | 42  | 23  | 8  | 11 | 82  | 41  | 77  |
| 1994-95:   | Premiership | 42  | 20  | 12 | 10 | 67  | 47  | 72  |
| 1995-96:   | Premiership | 38  | 24  | 6  | 8  | 66  | 37  | 78  |
| 1996-97:   | Premiership | 21  | 11  | 4  | 6  | 38  | 22  | 37  |
|            | Total       | 205 | 114 | 41 | 50 | 360 | 209 | 383 |

# THE BIG DEALS

## TRANSFERS OUT

### 1992

| | | |
|---|---|---|
| 20 Jul | Lee Makel (Blackburn) | £160,000 |
| 19 Dec | Peter Garland (Charlton) | undisclosed |
| 22 Dec | Mick Quinn (Coventry) | £250,000 |

### 1993

| | | |
|---|---|---|
| 26 Mar | Bjorn Kristensen (P'mth) | £120,000 |
| 8 Apr | Franz Carr (Sheff Utd) | undisclosed |
| 18 Jun | Andy Hunt (West Brom) | £100,000 |
| 23 Jun | David Kelly (Wolves) | £750,000 |
| 23 Jul | Mark Stimson (P'mth) | £100,000 |
| 5 Aug | Alan Thompson (Bolton) | £250,000 |
| 12 Aug | Gavin Peacock (Chelsea) | £1.25 million |
| 24 Sep | Tommy Wright (Nott For) | £450,000 |
| 1 Oct | David Roche (Doncaster) | exchange |

## 1994

| | | |
|---|---|---|
| 20 Jan | Brian Kilcline (Swindon) | £100,000 |
| 21 Jan | Liam O'Brien (Tranmere) | £300,000 |
| 1 Feb | Kevin Scott (Tottenham) | £850,000 |
| 16 Jun | Matt Appleby (Darlington) | free |
| 19 Jun | Alun Armstrong (Stockport) | £35,000 |
| 22 Jul | Mark Robinson (Swindon) | £600,000 |
| 25 Nov | Steve Guppy (Port Vale) | £225,000 |
| 16 Dec | Nico Papavasiliov (Ofi, Crete) | £25,000 |

## 1995

| | | |
|---|---|---|
| 12 Jan | Andy Cole (Man Utd) | £6.25 million |
| 24 Feb | Alex Mathie (Ipswich) | £500,000 |
| 23 Mar | Jason Drysdale (Swindon) | £340,000 |
| 23 May | Paul Bracewell (Sunderland) | £25,000 |
| 1 Jun | Alan Neilson (S'hampton) | £500,000 |
| 22 Jun | Michael Jeffrey (Rotherham) | £100,000 |
| 26 Jun | Barry Venison (Galatasaray) | £750,000 |
| 6 Oct | Ruel Fox (Tottenham) | £4.2 million |
| 7 Dec | Scott Sellars (Bolton) | £750,000 |

## 1996

| | | |
|---|---|---|
| 7 Mar | Marc Hottiger (Everton) | £700,000 |
| 25 Oct | Chris Holland (Birmingham) | £600,000 |
| 22 Nov | Darren Huckerby (Coventry) | £1 million |
| | *Total* | £21,280,000 |

# THE BIG DEALS

## TRANSFERS IN

### 1992

| | | |
|---|---|---|
| 20 Feb | Kevin Sheedy (Everton) | free |
| 20 Mar | Darren McDonough (Luton) | £90,000 |
| 20 Mar | Brian Kilcline (Oldham) | £250,000 |
| 24 Mar | Peter Garland (Tottenham) | £35,000 |
| 16 Jun | Paul Bracewell (Sunderland) | £250,000 |
| 2 Jul | John Beresford (Portsmouth) | £650,000 |
| 31 Jul | Barry Venison (Liverpool) | £250,000 |
| 22 Sep | Robert Lee (Charlton) | £700,000 |

### 1993

| | | |
|---|---|---|
| 9 Mar | Mark Robinson (Barnsley) | £450,000 |
| 9 Mar | Scott Sellars (Leeds) | £700,000 |
| 12 Mar | Andy Cole (Bristol City) | £1.75 million |
| 16 Jul | Peter Beardsley (Everton) | £1.5 million |
| 24 Jul | Nico Papavasiliou (Ofi, Crete) | £120,000 |
| 26 Jul | Alex Mathie (Morton) | £250,000 |
| 23 Sep | Michael Hooper (Liverpool) | £550,000 |
| 4 Oct | Michael Jeffrey (Doncaster) | £60,000 plus player |

# 1994

| | | |
|---|---|---|
| 20 Jan | Chris Holland (Preston) | £100,000 |
| 2 Feb | Ruel Fox (Norwich) | £2.25 million |
| 24 Mar | Darren Peacock (QPR) | £2.7 million |
| 25 Jul | Marc Hottiger (Sion) | £600,000 |
| 2 Aug | Steve Guppy (Wycombe) | £150,000 |
| 3 Aug | Jason Drysdale (Watford) | £425,000 |
| 10 Aug | Philippe Albert (Anderlecht) | £2.7 million |
| 26 Sep | Paul Kitson (Derby) | £2.25 million |

# 1995

| | | |
|---|---|---|
| 10 Jan | Keith Gillespie (Man Utd) | £1 million |
| | Jimmy Crawford (Bohemians) | £75,000 |
| 7 Jun | Warren Barton (Wimbledon) | £4 million |
| 9 Jun | Les Ferdinand (QPR) | £6 million |
| 6 Jul | David Ginola (Paris St G) | £2.5 million |
| 11 Aug | Shaka Hislop (Reading) | £1.575 million |
| 10 Nov | Darren Huckerby (Lincoln) | £500,000 |

# 1996

| | | |
|---|---|---|
| 8 Feb | Faustino Asprilla (Parma) | £7.5 million |
| 6 Mar | David Batty (Blackburn) | £3.75 million |
| 30 Jul | Alan Shearer (Blackburn) | £15 million |
| | *Total* | £60,960,000 |

# MANAGERS' RECORDS: LEAGUE (%)

| Managers | Home | | | | Away | |
|---|---|---|---|---|---|---|
| | P | W | D | L | P | W |
| | No. | % | % | % | No. | % |
| Ardiles O. | 21 | 33.33 | 43 | 24 | 20 | 5 |
| Charlton J. | 21 | 52.38 | 19 | 29 | 21 | 9.5 |
| Committee | 674 | 61.57 | 18 | 20 | 674 | 26 |
| Cox A. | 81 | 64.2 | 22 | 14 | 82 | 24 |
| Cunningham A. | 94 | 56.38 | 22 | 21 | 94 | 28 |
| Dinnis R. | 16 | 56.25 | 13 | 31 | 17 | 12 |
| Harvey J. | 273 | 54.95 | 26 | 19 | 273 | 21 |
| Harvey J. (C) | 1 | 100 | | | | |
| Keegan J.K. | 103 | 69.90 | 19 | 11 | 102 | 41 |
| Lee G. | 31 | 58.06 | 23 | 19 | 31 | 19 |
| Livingstone D. | 24 | 66.67 | 17 | 17 | 23 | 26 |
| Martin G. | 54 | 68.52 | 15 | 17 | 54 | 30 |
| Mather T. | 84 | 58.33 | 18 | 24 | 84 | 30 |
| McFaul I. | 67 | 47.76 | 24 | 28 | 67 | 19 |
| McFaul I. (C) | 2 | | 100 | | 2 | |
| McGarry W. | 58 | 50 | 26 | 24 | 57 | 14 |
| Mitten C. | 49 | 48.98 | 18 | 33 | 49 | 33 |
| Saxton R. (C) | | | | | 1 | |
| Seymour S. | 125 | 51.2 | 20 | 29 | 126 | 30 |
| Smith J. | 52 | 48.08 | 31 | 21 | 52 | 27 |
| Smith N. | 35 | 40 | 31 | 29 | 35 | 20 |
| Suggett C./ Martin M. (C) | 2 | | 50 | 50 | 2 | |
| Totals | 1867 | 57.74 | 21 | 21 | 1866 | 25 |

172

| Away | | Neutral | | | | Home and Away | | | |
|---|---|---|---|---|---|---|---|---|---|
| D | L | P | W | D | L | P | W | D | L |
| % | % | No. | % | % | % | No. | % | % | % |
| 35 | 60 | | | | | 41 | 19.5 | 39.0 | 41.5 |
| 43 | 47.62 | | | | | 42 | 31 | 31 | 38.1 |
| 24 | 50.59 | | | | | 1348 | 43.7 | 20.9 | 35.4 |
| 29 | 46.34 | | | | | 163 | 44.2 | 25.8 | 30.1 |
| 12 | 60.64 | | | | | 188 | 42.0 | 17.0 | 41 |
| 24 | 64.71 | | | | | 33 | 33.3 | 18.2 | 48.5 |
| 26 | 53.11 | | | | | 546 | 37.7 | 26.2 | 36.1 |
| | | | | | | 1 | 100 | | |
| 21 | 38.24 | | | | | 205 | 55.6 | 20 | 24.4 |
| 26 | 54.84 | | | | | 62 | 38.7 | 24.2 | 37.1 |
| 13 | 60.87 | | | | | 47 | 46.8 | 14.9 | 38.3 |
| 33 | 37.04 | | | | | 108 | 49.1 | 24.1 | 26.9 |
| 17 | 53.57 | | | | | 168 | 44.0 | 17.3 | 38.7 |
| 34 | 46.27 | | | | | 134 | 33.6 | 29.1 | 37.3 |
| 50 | 50 | | | | | 4 | | 75 | 25 |
| 28 | 57.89 | | | | | 115 | 32.2 | 27 | 40.9 |
| 14 | 53.06 | | | | | 98 | 40.8 | 16.3 | 42.9 |
| | 100 | | | | | 1 | | | 100 |
| 29 | 41.27 | | | | | 251 | 40.6 | 24.3 | 35.1 |
| 33 | 40.38 | | | | | 104 | 37.5 | 31.7 | 30.8 |
| 20 | 60 | | | | | 70 | 30 | 25.7 | 44.3 |
| | 100 | | | | | 4 | | 25 | 75 |
| 24 | 50.2 | | | | | 3733 | 41.5 | 22.9 | 35.6 |

# MANAGERS' RECORDS: LEAGUE AND CUP (%)

| Managers | Home | | | | Away | |
|---|---|---|---|---|---|---|
| | P | W | D | L | P | W |
| | No. | % | % | % | No. | % |
| Ardiles O. | 23 | 34.78 | 43 | 22 | 23 | 8.7 |
| Charlton J. | 24 | 50 | 17 | 33 | 24 | 13 |
| Committee | 740 | 61.89 | 18 | 20 | 725 | 27 |
| Cox A. | 90 | 60 | 23 | 17 | 89 | 25 |
| Cunningham A. | 100 | 57 | 22 | 21 | 100 | 27 |
| Dinnis R. | 19 | 52.63 | 11 | 37 | 19 | 11 |
| Harvey J. | 306 | 54.90 | 26 | 19 | 315 | 22 |
| Harvey J. (C) | 1 | 100 | | | 1 | |
| Keegan J.K. | 124 | 70.97 | 19 | 9.7 | 125 | 40 |
| Lee G. | 41 | 63.41 | 20 | 17 | 41 | 20 |
| Livingstone D. | 28 | 67.86 | 18 | 14 | 28 | 32 |
| Martin G. | 55 | 67.27 | 15 | 18 | 55 | 29 |
| Mather T. | 88 | 57.95 | 18 | 24 | 91 | 30 |
| McFaul I. | 77 | 50.65 | 22 | 27 | 74 | 18 |
| McFaul I. (C) | 2 | | 100 | | 2 | |
| McGarry W. | 65 | 49.23 | 28 | 23 | 62 | 13 |
| Mitten C. | 51 | 47.06 | 20 | 33 | 51 | 31 |
| Saxton R. (C) | | | | | 1 | |
| Seymour S. | 137 | 52.55 | 20 | 27 | 139 | 34 |
| Smith J. | 61 | 47.54 | 31 | 21 | 59 | 25 |
| Smith N. | 42 | 42.86 | 26 | 31 | 36 | 19 |
| Suggett C./ | | | | | | |
| Martin M. (C) | 2 | | 50 | 50 | 2 | |
| Totals | 2076 | 57.95 | 21 | 21 | 2062 | 26 |

174

| Away | | Neutral | | | | Home and Away | | | |
|---|---|---|---|---|---|---|---|---|---|
| D | L | P | W | D | L | P | W | D | L |
| % | % | No. | % | % | % | No. | % | % | % |
| 35 | 56.52 | | | | | 46 | 21.7 | 39.1 | 39.1 |
| 46 | 41.67 | | | | | 48 | 31.3 | 31.3 | 37.5 |
| 24 | 49.66 | 17 | 53 | 18 | 29 | 1482 | 44.5 | 20.9 | 34.5 |
| 28 | 47.19 | | | | | 179 | 42.5 | 25.7 | 31.8 |
| 13 | 60 | 3 | 100 | | | 203 | 42.9 | 17.2 | 39.9 |
| 26 | 63.16 | | | | | 38 | 31.6 | 18.4 | 50 |
| 25 | 53.33 | 4 | 50 | 25 | 25 | 625 | 38.1 | 25.4 | 36.5 |
| | 100 | | | | | 2 | 50 | | 50 |
| 21 | 39.2 | | | | | 249 | 55.4 | 20.1 | 24.5 |
| 32 | 48.78 | 2 | 50 | | 50 | 84 | 41.7 | 25 | 33.3 |
| 18 | 50 | 3 | 67 | 33 | | 59 | 50.8 | 18.6 | 30.5 |
| 33 | 38.18 | | | | | 110 | 48.2 | 23.6 | 28.2 |
| 18 | 52.75 | | | | | 179 | 43.6 | 17.9 | 38.5 |
| 32 | 50 | | | | | 151 | 34.4 | 27.2 | 38.4 |
| 50 | 50 | | | | | 4 | | 75 | 25 |
| 29 | 58.06 | | | | | 127 | 31.5 | 28.3 | 40.2 |
| 14 | 54.90 | | | | | 102 | 39.2 | 16.7 | 44.1 |
| | 100 | | | | | 1 | | | 100 |
| 27 | 39.57 | 7 | 57 | 29 | 14 | 283 | 43.5 | 23.7 | 32.9 |
| 32 | 42.37 | | | | | 120 | 36.7 | 31.7 | 31.7 |
| 22 | 58.33 | | | | | 78 | 32.1 | 24.4 | 43.6 |
| | 100 | | | | | 4 | | 25 | 75 |
| 24 | 49.7 | 36 | 58 | 19 | 22 | 4174 | 42.1 | 22.8 | 35.1 |

175

Keegan has the highest % of wins both home and away, and the lowest % of defeats at home. The record is only spoilt by Martin G. who only suffered 38.18% of away defeats as opposed to Keegan's 39.2%.